SPIRIT POSSESSION
AND EXORCISM

Spirit Possession and Exorcism: History, Psychology, and Neurobiology

Volume 1: Mental States and the Phenomenon of Possession
Volume 2: Rites to Become Possessed, Rites to Exorcise "Demons"

SPIRIT POSSESSION AND EXORCISM: HISTORY, PSYCHOLOGY, AND NEUROBIOLOGY

Volume 2:

Rites to Become Possessed, Rites to Exorcise "Demons"

Patrick McNamara

Brain, Behavior, and Evolution
Patrick McNamara, Series Editor

 PRAEGER

AN IMPRINT OF ABC-CLIO, LLC
Santa Barbara, California • Denver, Colorado • Oxford, England

Library of Congress Cataloging-in-Publication Data

McNamara, Patrick, 1956–
  Spirit possession and exorcism : history, psychology, and neurobiology /
Patrick McNamara.
    p. cm.
  Includes bibliographical references and index.
  ISBN 978-0-313-38432-5 (hardcopy : alk. paper)—ISBN 978-0-313-38433-2 (ebook)
  1. Spirit possession. 2. Demoniac possession. 3. Exorcism. I. Title.
  BL482.M36   2011
  204′.2—dc22   2010045373

ISBN 978-0-313-38432-5
EISBN 978-0-313-38433-2

15 14 13 12 11   1 2 3 4 5

This book is also available on the World Wide Web as an eBook.
Visit www.abc-clio.com for details.

Praeger
An Imprint of ABC-CLIO, LLC

ABC-CLIO, LLC
130 Cremona Drive, P.O. Box 1911
Santa Barbara, California 93116-1911

This book is printed on acid-free paper ∞

Manufactured in the United States of America

Case studies from Carrazana E., DeToledo J., Tatum W., et al. 1999. "Epilepsy and
Religious Experiences: Voodoo Possessions." *Epilepsia*, 40(2): 239–241. Used with
permission from John Wiley and Sons.

The exorcism ceremony is taken from Fr. Philip T. Weller. 2007. *The Roman
Ritual, Volume III: The Blessings*. Boonville, NY: Preserving Christian Publications.
Reprinted with permission from Preserving Christian Publications.

Every reasonable effort has been made to trace the owners of copyright materials
in this book, but in some instances this has proven impossible. The editors and
publishers will be glad to receive information leading to more complete
acknowledgments in subsequent printings of the book and in the meantime extend
their apologies for any omissions.

To Ina Livia McNamara and Reka Szent-Imrey

Contents

Contents

Series Foreword

Beginning in the 1990s, behavioral scientists—that is, people who study mind, brain, and behavior—began to take the theory of evolution seriously. They began to borrow techniques developed by the evolutionary biologists and apply them to problems in mind, brain, and behavior. Now, of course, virtually all behavioral scientists up to that time had claimed to endorse evolutionary theory, but few used it to study the problems they were interested in. All that changed in the 1990s. Since that pivotal decade, breakthroughs in the behavioral and brain sciences have been constant, rapid, and unremitting. The purpose of the Brain, Behavior, and Evolution series of titles published by ABC-CLIO is to bring these new breakthroughs in the behavioral sciences to the attention of the general public.

In the past decade, some of these scientific breakthroughs have come to inform the clinical and biomedical disciplines. That means that people suffering from all kinds of diseases and disorders, particularly brain and behavioral disorders, will benefit from these new therapies. That is exciting news indeed, and the general public needs to learn about these breakthrough findings and treatments. A whole new field called evolutionary medicine has begun to transform the way medicine is practiced and has led to new treatments and new approaches to diseases, like the dementias, sleep disorders, psychiatric diseases, and developmental disorders that seemed intractable to previous efforts. The series of books in the Brain, Behavior, and Evolution series seeks both to contribute to this new evolutionary approach to brain and behavior and to bring the insights emerging from the new evolutionary approaches to psychology, medicine, and anthropology to the general public.

The Brain, Behavior, and Evolution series was inspired by and brought to fruition with the help of Debora Carvalko at ABC-CLIO. The series editor,

Dr. Patrick McNamara, is the director of the Evolutionary Neurobehavior Laboratory in the Department of Neurology at Boston University School of Medicine. He has devoted most of his scientific work to development of an evolutionary approach to problems of sleep medicine and to neurodegenerative diseases. Titles in the series will focus on applied and clinical implications of evolutionary approaches to the whole range of brain and behavioral disorders. Contributions are solicited from leading figures in the fields of interest to the series. Each volume will cover the basics, define the terms, and analyze the full range of issues and findings relevant to the clinical disorder or topic that is the focus of the volume. Each volume will demonstrate how the application of evolutionary modes of analysis leads to new insights on causes of disorder and functional breakdowns in brain and behavior relationships. Each volume, furthermore, will be aimed at both popular and professional audiences and will be written in a style appropriate for the general reader, the local and university libraries, and graduate and undergraduate students. The publications that become part of this series will therefore bring the gold discovered by scientists using evolutionary methods to understand brain and behavior to the attention of the general public, and ultimately, it is hoped, to those families and individuals currently suffering from those most intractable of disorders—the brain and behavioral disorders.

Foreword

Humanity cannot be understood apart from religion and religion, I will argue in this book, cannot be understood apart from "spirit possession." "Spirit possession" is the taking over of an individual's sense of agency and identity by a supernatural agent. This "taking over" of the host's sense of agency and identity can be either a positive or a negative experience. When it is positive, the mind and personality of the possessed individual are transfigured and the individual seems to be acting more freely and effectively. A famous case involves one of the founders of Christianity, St. Paul. He claims in his letters to the early Christian communities that "I no longer live, but Christ lives in me."

In all cases of positive possession the new personality has left behind the old, the lower self, and now lives via a new transformed self linked to the divine consciousness and is in fact identified with this divine consciousness. The link to or bond with the divine consciousness seems to enhance perceptual capacities and intelligence and can produce some very fine character traits like gratitude, generosity, compassion for others, fearlessness, clear strategic sense, joy, and many other qualities besides. Clearly, any process that can enhance one's perceptual and information-processing capacities and give one these character traits must be transformative indeed and must be considered quite valuable—indeed priceless. That is why this form of possession, St. Paul calls it "putting on the Mind of Christ" (Rom. 12:2), is something all serious religious believers desire and act to acquire.

The negative form of possession, however, was and is an experience of a very different kind, though once again perceptual and information-processing capacities of the possessed individual are often enhanced, though this time not permanently. Negative possession is now known in many cultures as "demonic possession." In the ancient world negative forms of possession could occur with almost any sort of spirit entity, including many of the gods worshiped by the ancients as well as spirits of the dead, animal spirits, ancestor spirits, and all kinds of intermediate beings such as demi-gods, faeries, angels, mountain spirits, and many other types of beings as well. Although an individual undergoing demonic possession could often evidence unusual cognitive abilities like "reading the mind" of others, predicting future events, or having knowledge of foreign languages and the like, negative possession (I will call it "demonic possession" in this work) was an experience that was feared. It has to be ranked among the most unfortunate and perilous forms of suffering a human being can undergo. It is so perilous a condition that special rituals have been evolved over the centuries by most peoples—at least all those who have been studied to date—to rid the possessed of the demon or to prevent possession in the first place. I will discuss those rituals (including formal exorcism), along with the history, biology, and phenomenology of demonic possession in volume 2 of this work. In volume 1, I review the history of positive spirit possession and of religion itself from the period of the Upper Paleolithic right up to the present. I regard both positive and negative (demonic) forms of spirit possession to have their roots in the social complex of the "divine kingship"—the king who had to embody both the best of the community and the worst. The king renewed the community by collecting within himself all the sins and ritual impurities of the people into his divine person. Then the king was ritually sacrificed, thus eliminating ritual impurities from the community. When kings are for some reason not seen as fulfilling this service, vulnerable individuals from ordinary ranks of society take on the sacrificial role normally handled by the king, and this is what we call demonic possession.

In both positive and negative forms of spirit possession the individual identity or self comes face to face with a supernatural entity or agent. This face-to-face confrontation between the human "I" and the inhuman agent is experienced as uncanny, numinous, terrifying, and ultimate. It is a perilous boundary experience where one being, the human being, is turned into another being, a supernatural or a nonhuman being. It is a place or experience where the self is, for better or worse, transformed by religious forces. In this face-to-face confrontation or fight there is also a power exchange. If the human agent loses all control over the experience he becomes a plaything of the alien entity. He watches as the alien entity acts and acts most frequently with ferocious violence. If, on the other hand, the human agent wins the battle to control the influx of the supernatural energies, he becomes infused with extraordinary physical and mental powers that he can use himself rather than be used by them—powers that would make other people quake with fear in his presence. Spirit possession, therefore, was often a sought-after experience. It could confer prestige and power. But it was always understood to be risky, even perilous, and not to be undertaken frivolously. Because spirit possession was a source of power, the spiritual world began to be understood as a realm of fearsome power that needed to be dealt with with utmost care, seriousness, and circumspection. This fear of the power of the spirit world in relation to spirit possession is one source of ritual and sacrificial rites. Thus, spirit possession, in its relation with sacrifice, must be considered a phenomenon that lies at the heart of the religious experience and is therefore foundational to religion itself.

Preface

This project is a two-volume work on spirit possession. Volume 1 focuses on positive and controlled forms of spirit possession while volume 2 focuses on negative, uncontrolled and "demonic" possession states and related exorcism rituals. I look at the history of religions from the point of view of spirit-possession experiences. I argue that spirit-possession phenomena has decisively influenced religious practices right from the beginnings of religion itself which I locate in the middle Paleolithic period. Spirit-possession experiences shaped religious consciousness and behaviors for millenia because possession experiences decisively shaped cultural constructs of what counts as knowledge and of identity and the self. Positive, controlled spirit-possession rituals reached their peak in a cultural phenomenon that anthropologists have called the divine or sacred kingship. In the social and cultural complex called divine kingship the king is treated as the embodiment of a high god interested in power, mercy, and justice for his people. The king modeled for his people the highest possible development of the human character for the culture he governed. Controlled spirit-possession techniques were used to facilitate that sort of character development. These sacred kings were also assumed to unavoidably collect all the evils and impurities of the people because they were the only individuals who formed the connecting bond between all the people in the realm. All were subject to the king and the king was therefore exposed to all the sins of the people. These evils had to be eliminated from the community—often by ritually killing the king himself. The king became the scapegoat for the people and this mechanism for the elimination of impurities or the expiation of sins, rooted as it was in the divine kingship, became one of the source mechanisms for the core exorcism rituals found throughout the world. Ecstatic possession cults capitalized on uncontrolled possession states to foster creation of mock "kings" or mock victims that mimicked the expiation rituals around the sacred kingship. Whatever the root sources of demonic possession the experiences of those possessed are taken seriously in volume 2 of this work. A psychology, neurology, and history of demonic possession and of the people who undergo these terrible experiences is attempted in volume 2. Volume 1 demonstrates that some shamans, men's secret societies, and sacred kings developed techniques to control spirit-possession experience. Volume 2 examines the consequences of attempts to utilize spirit-possession rituals by the uninitiated and in an uncontrolled way.

Acknowledgments

I would like to thank Debbie Carvalko from ABC-CLIO for suggesting this topic to me as worthy of a separate study. Thank you to Debbie also for her patience in seeing the project to completion. I would also like to thank Emily Abrams, Andrea Avalos, Jessica Ghofrani, Katherine Hendley, and Michael Josephs for their help in tracking down references for these volumes and for their assistance with the typing and scoring of cases of demonic possession, a thankless task at best, but these assistants did it both conscientiously and carefully. I would especially like to thank Emily, Andrea, and Michael for the scoring of phenomenologic elements of the possession case studies. I thank Drs. Raymon Durso, Sanford Auerbach, and Wesley Wildman for many discussions on the psychology of religion as well as their support and guidance over many years. I would like to extend a special thanks to Ms. Erica Harris, my head Research Coordinator, who helped out on all aspects of this book project—all while expertly managing a lab and office crew each day. Thanks also go to the support of the Institute for the Biocultural Study of Religion (IBCSR).

Chapter 1

Introduction to Second Volume: The Roots of the Demonic Possession Experience

Sometime in July of 2009 police were called to a house in San Antonio, Texas. Newspaper reports at the time said that "the scene was so gruesome investigators could barely speak: A 3½-week-old boy lay dismembered in the bedroom of a single-story house, three of his tiny toes chewed off, his face torn away, his head severed and his brains ripped out. . . . Officers found the boy's mother, Otty Sanchez, sitting on the couch with a self-inflicted wound to her chest and her throat partially slashed, screaming, 'I killed my baby! I killed my baby!' She told officers the devil made her do it, police said" (Weber 2009).

It later emerged that Otty had reported hearing voices, including the voice of Satan telling her to kill her baby and then to eat his body parts (Associated Press 2009). She had been diagnosed with both schizophrenia and post-partum depression. She appears to have believed she was possessed by Satan. The latter belief is all too common in schizophrenics with religious delusions.

Schizophrenia is a disorder of the self, involving psychotic delusions and hallucination, which usually has its onset during the adolescent period. As was the case with Sanchez, there is a definite heightening of religiousness in many schizophrenic patients (Huguelet et al. 2006; Mohr et al. 2006; Siddle et al. 2002). In a sample of 193 patients admitted to a community hospital for schizophrenia, 24% had more than just a "heightening" of religiosity; instead, they evidenced outright religious delusions (Siddle et al. 2002). Many of these religious delusions are actually demonic in nature—that is, they are "command" delusions where patients feel they are being commanded by a demon to hurt themselves or others, including their own children. It appears, then, that certain forms of brain disorder, such as schizophrenia, can contribute to demonic possession.

It is important, however, not to pathologize demonic possession experiences prematurely. In fact, there is usually little or no evidence for brain or personality disorders in people who report demonic possession experiences (see review in DePalatis 2006). In a study by Kua, Sim, and Chee (1986), 36 young men in Singapore who presented to a psychiatric service with possession-trance were followed up for four to five years. Twenty-six were studied on follow-up after five years. None of these patients showed any evidence of psychiatric illness on follow-up. Thus, possession may not be a form of mental illness. It must be considered a religious form of suffering that mimics mental illness in the majority of cases and that can be associated with overt brain disorder in some cases.

Some investigators have suggested that the majority of cases of demonic possession can be considered neuroses in the Freudian sense while more extreme cases can be considered psychoses. For patients with possession who are firmly attached to a religious tradition, effective treatment may be available in the form of exorcism rituals. Of course one should always employ all standard forms of biomedical treatment for treatment of neuroses but when all standard forms of biomedical therapy do not help, religious rituals can be ethically attempted, it seems to me. It is therefore unethical and unwise to tell a religious patient who reports intense suffering from a possession experience that exorcism rituals are bunk and that religious tools are useless.

So if negative or demonic possession cannot be ascribed to mental disorder, what then is its root cause and what is its essential nature and function? Long before Oesterreich (1922/1974) compiled the existing literature on possession and discussed it within a naturalistic framework, the ancient Greek tragedians explored the root mechanisms of demonic possession in their plays and tragedies. They, in my view, give us the first true insight into the driving mechanisms behind demonic possession as they link demonic possession with defects in the institution of the divine kingship (or, more often, in the king himself), violence, and religious sacrifice.

The tragedians wrote and performed their plays at the festival of Dionysus (the Dionysia) under the sign of Dionysus, the Greek god of wine and ecstasy. Cultic rites associated with Dionysus sometimes included manifestations of group frenzy such as screams and vocalizations, maniacal dancing, and sexual acts. Members of the cult were most often women and were called maenads or Bacchae (literally "raving ones"). The maenads would dress in fawn skins and carry a thyrsus, a long stick wrapped in ivy or vine leaves and tipped by a cluster of leaves. The Dionysian rites usually climaxed in the frenzied mutilation of anything standing nearby such as trees, shrubs, or even manmade structures. All too often the rites involved the manic dismemberment of living animals. A bull was preferred as the bull was the symbol of Dionysus. But that must have been a rare event, given the expense of slaughtering a bull. After tearing the animal to pieces (*sparagmos*) the maenads would drench themselves in its flesh and blood and eat its raw bloody flesh (*omophagia*).

EURIPIDES' *BACCHAE*

Toward the end of his life Euripides became interested in the bloody rites of the maenads and wrote *The Bacchae*. The play begins with reports that the Bacchae are acting up again. They have been appearing in public with snakes in their hair, and suckling wild wolves and gazelles. The women rove in bands; one band of drunken or crazed women had descended on a herd of cows, ripping them to shreds with their bare hands. Thus the bizarre conduct of the cult's members has led to destruction of property and the king must act. King Pentheus appears, therefore, to be acting reasonably when trying to reign in the maenads' destructive practices. But the god Dionysus refuses to see his cult suppressed and he lays a plot to destroy Pentheus. So he goes to Pentheus in disguise and talks Pentheus into self-destruction. Note that the king had to have had a spiritual weakness that the god could exploit if the god was to be successful in opposing the king's meager efforts at suppression of the god's cult. The god knows that Pentheus is secretly fascinated with these ecstatic rites. The stories he is told about the women involved seem fantastic. His own mother, the queen, is a devotee of Dionysus and apparently participates in the maenads' frenzied rites. Even Pentheus's grandfather, Cadmus, speaks enthusiastically about the cult. Thus the god disguised as a stranger bringing news of the maenads' ecstatic practices uses Pentheus's curiosity and deep desire to see the ecstatic women to lead Pentheus to his own self-destruction.

Stranger: Ah! Would you like to see them in their gatherings upon the mountain?
Pentheus: Very much. Ay, and pay uncounted gold for the pleasure.
Stranger: Why have you conceived so strong a desire?
Pentheus: Though it would pain me to see them drunk with wine-
Stranger: Yet you would like to see them, pain and all?

Pentheus never answers Dionysus's question as to *why* he wants to witness the women's rites. We do not learn why Pentheus has conceived so strong a desire to see the crazed women. That the king should be interested in them is understood. As mentioned, these women have been disturbing the peace of the realm. His own family has become involved with them. But why should the king want to *see* them during their rites? The play seems to suggest that the king suffers from a divided consciousness and a spiritual weakness. Not only does Pentheus *not* want to see them during their rites he even claims that it would cause him pain to see them, including his own mother, behaving like crazed animals. Yet Pentheus finds himself saying that he strongly desires to see them, pain and all. King Pentheus's divided consciousness shows the audience that there is something rotten in the kingship itself.

Once he has effectively exploited Pentheus's weaknesses the god moves to destroy the kingship itself via the destruction of the house of the king—Pentheus and his royal family. The god proceeds to systematically strip the king of dignity and rationality. The god decides to humiliate Pentheus by having him dress as a woman. He convinces the king to dress as a female maenad to avoid detection by the other maenads and thus be able to observe the rites without molestation. Dionysus balks at this further humiliation: "Nay; am I a woman, then, And no man more?" Dionysus points out that if he is seen by the maenads to be a man they will kill him: "Would ye have them slay thee dead? No man may see their mysteries" and live. Pentheus then consents to being dressed as a woman and a maenad and in doing so is led inexorably to his own destruction. Dionysus dresses Pentheus as a woman and gives him a thyrsus and fawn skins, then leads him out into the streets to be mocked. Pentheus begins to see double, and hallucinates two bulls (Dionysus often took the form of a bull) leading him. The scene switches back to the palace where a messenger reports to Cadmus that Pentheus has been killed. He recounts the story of what happened to the tragic king: When the stranger and the king reached Cithaeron, the site where the rites were underway, the blond stranger helped the king climb atop a tree to view the rites. Then the stranger manifested as the god in all his glory and Dionysus called out to his followers that a man was watching them. This, of course, drove the maenads wild with rage, and they pulled the trapped Pentheus down and ripped his body to pieces.

After the messenger has relayed this grievous news to Cadmus, Pentheus' mother, Agave, arrives, carrying the head of her son. She thinks that the head is the head of a mountain lion. She had killed the "lion," she boasts, with her bare hands and pulled his head off. Then in the most macabre and tragic scene imaginable, she proudly displays her son's head to her father Cadmus, the grandfather of the slain son, believing it to be a hunting trophy. She is confused when Cadmus does not delight in her "success" and hunting prowess. By that time, however, Dionysus's possession of Agave is beginning to wear off, and as Cadmus reels from the horror of his grandson's grisly death at the hands of his own mother, Agave slowly realizes what she has done.

WHAT WE CAN LEARN ABOUT DEMONIC POSSESSION FROM *THE BACCHAE*

Euripides' play gives us some helpful clues to help unlock the mysteries of spirit possession, particularly demonic possession. First, the play tells us that the release of the demonic is linked to the breakdown in the complex system of divine kingship. When the kingship is weak the public sacrificial rites are seen by the people as less effective and they therefore turn to other means to expiate anxiety, guilt, transgressions, and the like. The play also points to female sex as more vulnerable to demonic infestation when the public sacrificial rites are ineffective due to a weak kingship. The play suggests that to the degree that the sense of personal agency is impaired in people due to the possession experience (exemplified in the maenads), extraordinary physical strength and various forms of violence become possible in the person who is possessed. Through the centuries extraordinary strength has been noted by clerics and doctors as a reliable sign of demonic possession. Violent language, acts, and sentiments have also been constants. In *The Bacchae*, the possessed exhibit the strength to uproot trees and in an ecstasy of violent rage dismember an onlooker merely because he is male and without stopping to identify him first.

The Bacchae also alerts us to the importance of group possession, where all members of a small group undergo possession. In this type of possession group synchrony in action becomes more reliable. In *The Bacchae* the possessed group consisted of women behaving in frenzied and ecstatic ways. When men become possessed it is not usually seen as part of a group phenomenon. Even when ancient male warriors were preparing for face-to-face combat in war they tended not to opt for group possession but instead preferred individualized possession. Men, furthermore, are not supposed to witness these group female religious rites.

These male-female differences in possession experience point to more fundamental biologic differences in the sexes as one source for possession phenomena. To illustrate: Chris Knight (1991) and others have suggested that one source of group behavior and coalitional alliances among females (such as synchronized menstruation) lies in adoption by females of an evolutionary strategy that seeks to manipulate males into provisioning all females (and offspring) in a tribe or clan with resources. If all females in a tribal group advertise sexual receptivity, then none can be singled out for special treatment by males. If males do not know which children are theirs, they are less likely to kill infants and children that may not be fathered by them (as is all too often the case among our primate ancestors). Female coalitions can also prevent males from killing infants. In extreme cases females will gang up on a violent male and eliminate him. Female group religious rites might therefore function in part to protect offspring and sometimes that protection will lead to group killing of dangerous males. Alternatively group violence by females may be directed at outgroup raiders, males from other tribes who come to rape and kill. Whatever the functions of group behaviors among females, it is important to note that group behavior was probably facilitated by possession trance in ancestral females. Possession involves a reduction in self-determination and an enhancement in Other-determination.

The Bacchae also suggests that possession can be studied in part as a phenomenon of inheritance or an intergenerational transmission of proclivities, behaviors, and "sins." Generation 1, represented by Cadmus the grandfather, is fascinated with the maenads and their rites. Generation 2, represented by Agave, actually participates in the rites. Generation 3, represented by Pentheus, pays the price of that participation. Pentheus is even more fascinated with the rites than is Cadmus but Pentheus becomes the sacrificial victim to the rites. An interest in possession leads to possession and possession leads to sacrificial violence. Perhaps the function of possession has something to do with sacrificial violence—at least when we are considering female religious rites. In generation 1 the alien entity that will enact the possession announces itself. In generation 2 it accomplishes the possession, and by generation 3 it has accomplished its purpose. On the face of it, if we take the example of the Bacchae to be truly representative of violent female possession rites then one of its purposes appears to be the elimination of male offspring.

I wish to pursue this line of thought a little further. We will see later that genetic elements that have an evolutionary or fitness interest in eliminating male offspring are, in fact, implicated as well in brain states that can arguably support possession.

GENETIC ROOTS OF DEMONIC POSSESSION IN FEMALES

In the tragic case of Otty Sanchez and in the case of *The Bacchae*, spirit possession was associated with maternal killing of male offspring. The demon that possessed Otty Sanchez killed her baby, "Scotty." We can rule out the idea that Otty Sanchez was simply a sadistic killer who tried to avert responsibility for the gruesome murder by claiming "The devil made me do it." No, Otty Sanchez was psychotic. It is important to note Otty Sanchez did not kill other children who were sleeping in a room next to hers that terrible night. Sanchez killed only her baby and then tried to kill herself. She did not try to kill the other children (children of her sister). If she was merely a sadistic murderer, the killing would not have ceased with the death of her child.

Unfortunately, infanticide by mothers is a relatively common occurrence in human culture. It has always existed, whether condoned or not condoned by authorities. Other species, including our relatives the nonhuman primates, practice infanticide. Primate mothers, when they kill their offspring, not infrequently eat part of the bodies (often the brains) of those offspring. Apparently under certain ecologic conditions, extreme conditions of famine and the like, it does not "pay" to raise offspring. Under those conditions reproductive systems and behaviors are inhibited and other more gruesome behavioral strategies are triggered to eliminate the young. Was the psychosis in the case of Otty Sanchez and her baby due to local ecologic conditions somehow dire enough to trigger infanticide? We will never know. But once again it is worth noting that Otty's infant was male and that the person killed and eaten by his own mother in *The Bacchae* was also male—King Pentheus.

It is worth following this strand of evidence concerning effects of demonic possession in females for a bit. From a biologic point of view one potential source of these sorts of demonic commands to hurt one's male offspring is genomic, that is, groups of genes that are transmitted solely down the female line and that are "interested" in eliminating genes that are transmitted down the male line.

Organisms are composed of multiple genetic entities that do not always share the same interests because they have different modes of inheritance. Different transmission patterns of genes to offspring create the context for conflict or negative fitness covariance between two associated or antagonistic genes. For example, genes that are normally passed on by only one sex, such as mitochondrial genes inherited through the female line, differ in their transmission patterns from Y-chromosome genes inherited through the male line, and can therefore enter into conflict with them. Mitochondrial genes can only be passed along via females and so these genes have devised mechanisms to create more females and to eliminate males—especially when resources are scarce. Similarly, Y-chromosome genes can only be passed along in the male line and so they are interested only in producing males and in eliminating females. Sykes (2003) has suggested that these genetic "interests" may be one reason why some families consist of only daughters over several generations or only sons over several generations.

The genetic tug of war between male and female line genomes may help to explain variations in sexual orientation as well as why females and some males are more likely to report possession phenomena. Recall that in *The Bacchae* the god humiliated King Pentheus by having him dress in women's clothes. Current theory concerning transexualism invokes genetic conflict between male and female genes (Green and Keverne 2000). A significant skewing in the sex ratio in favor of females has been reported for the families of homosexual men such that there are fewer maternal uncles than aunts. This difference in the genealogical sex ratio could be due to effects of mitochondria operating through neuroendo- crine mechanisms to eliminate or feminize male offspring. Another poten- tial explanation involves genomic imprinting. Green and Keverne (2000) assessed 417 male-to-female transsexuals and 96 female-to-male transsex- uals. Like male homosexuals, male-to-female transsexuals were found to have a significant excess of maternal aunts versus uncles. No differences from the expected parity were found for female-to-male transsexuals or on the paternal side. Green and Keverne suggested that aberrant forms of X inactivation and imprinting of selected genes on the X chromosome may help to explain these findings. Females carry two X chromosomes, one inherited from the father and one from the mother. Normally one of these X chromosomes is inactivated by the gene Xist and females "use" the other functional X chromosome. Green and Keverne hypothesized that in families that produce homosexuals imprinting mechanisms influence the X chromosome inherited from the father. In generation 1 there is a failure to erase the paternal imprints on the paternal X chromosome so the pater- nal X chromosome is not fully functional in offspring. Daughters who are carriers of this aberrant paternal X in generation 2 would therefore pro- duce sons in generation 3 that are XpY and XmY. Since XpY expresses Xist (the gene that inactivates the extra X chromosome in females), the X chromosome is silenced and half of the sons are lost at the earliest stages of pregnancy because of the normal requirement for paternal X expression in extra-embryonic tissues (females survive by virtue of inheriting two X chromosomes and are thus ultimately overrepresented in the geneology). Surviving sons inherit the feminizing Xp-imprinted genes. These sons become homosexual or transsexual.

Another way in which the intergenerational battle of the sexes is carried on genetically is via transmission of parasites. Parasites and their hosts each use genes transmitted via male or female lines to accomplish their selfish ends. The host evolves mechanisms to reduce the damage inflicted by the parasite, and the parasite evolves adaptations to extract resources from the host, despite the host's countermeasures, to improve the chances that its descendants will be transmitted to infect new hosts. Some parasites, such as certain microsporidians in mosquitoes, are only transmitted through females (in the egg cytoplasm). When these parasites find themselves in males, they kill the host and try to get to an alternative host (typically a copepod). In females (daughters) the parasites are harmless. Similarly, in some crustaceans, cytoplasmic bacteria called Wolbachia turn males into females and exploit the "female" to find new hosts to infect.

Another form of genetic conflict, called *meiotic drive*, occurs when a gene obtains, during meiosis, a transmission advantage. Meiotic drive can involve both the sex chromosomes and the autosomes. *Segregation distortion* is a form of autosomal meiotic drive that has been intensively studied in the fruit fly, *Drosophila melanogaster*. A similar driving system characterizes the t locus on chromosome 17 in mice. The products of the genes encoded at the t locus are necessary for normal spermatogenesis, and thus when the males come to maturity they are sterile.

Another form of intragenomic conflict that involves an intergenerational battle between the sexes is called *genomic imprinting*. Genomic imprinting refers to the silencing of one allele of a gene according to its parental origin. The silencing or tagging of the DNA probably involves methylation of CpG-rich domains. Thus, each cell in the progeny recognizes and expresses only one allele of a gene locus, namely either the paternally derived or the maternally derived allele. The pattern-specific monoallelic expression of imprinted genes results in a bias in the inheritance of traits, with some traits inherited down the matriline and others down the patriline. Most of the genes identified to date as imprinted code for proteins that influence early growth, with paternally expressed loci increasing and maternally expressed loci restraining allocation of resources by the mother to her offspring.

Haig and colleagues (Haig, 2000, 2002; Haig and Westoby 1988) conceptualized the evolution of genomic imprinting in terms of a process of genetic conflict between the maternal and paternal genomes that obtains whenever there is uncertainty about paternity of offspring (which is considered to be the case for human biology). Because a paternal gene in one offspring is unlikely to be in its siblings or its mother, the paternal gene can increase its chances of getting into the next generation (i.e., its fitness) if it promotes extraction of resources from the mother regardless of costs to the mother or its siblings, who, in the context of paternity uncertainty, may carry genes of another male parent. The maternal gene, by contrast, is in all the siblings and thus its fitness is increased by favoring cooperation and sharing of resources.

Evolutionary conflict can also occur among the autosomal genes of mother and offspring. Trivers (1974) pointed out that parent-offspring conflict, while not a form of intragenomic conflict, likely influences a number of traits in mammalian life histories. Parents and offspring share only 50% of their genes. Thus there is plenty of room for conflict. Parental expenditure of time and resources on one offspring has an opportunity cost that means less time and fewer resources are available for other (perhaps future) offspring. Offspring are predicted to attempt to acquire more parental investment and resources than parents are selected to supply. Parent-offspring conflict arises because genes expressed in offspring will evolve to discount benefits and costs to a parent's residual reproductive value relative to costs and benefits to the offspring's reproductive value.

All of these forms of genetic conflict likely impact brain and behavioral processes in ways that are crucial for understanding possession phenomena. In the cases of *The Bacchae* and Otty and Scotty Sanchez, a radically reductionistic and genetic account of the tragedies would suggest that genetic elements that are transmitted down the female line (e.g., the mitochondrial DNA) have shaped selected and facultative behavioral strategies in a way that will eliminate male offspring. Now this reductionistic account of the tragedies, while interesting, cannot be the whole story. We have seen that in both *The Bacchae* and the Otty Sanchez tragedies possession by a supernatural agent was necessary in order to violently eliminate male offspring. It will therefore be necessary to explore the psychologic and cognitive dynamics of possession state in detail before we can arrive at a more satisfactory understanding of the nature and function of possession states. We will also need to explore the links between possession states and religious sacrifice more generally.

Even if we take a radically reductionistic stance on possession and the tragedies associated with demonic possession, genetic conflict turns out to be about much more than a mere battle between the sexes. Yes, one source of the killing by a mother of her own male offspring is sexual genetic conflict, but genetic conflict also gives rise to all kinds of cooperative groups that are internally benign but externally ferocious toward members of outgroups. The maenads are a group and when possessed by the god their function becomes manifest: to violently kill nonmembers such as animals and males. This sort of group programming is not mere killing for killing's sake. It is also defensive in nature. If our ancestors did not learn to kill cooperatively, in groups, they would have been killed themselves, along with everyone in their families and tribe. Such has been the condition of humankind for millennia: kill or be killed.

Once again, however, this is not the whole story. When cooperative groups become larger and more inclusive, they tend to temper the ferocious violence directed against outgroups under certain, very limited circumstances. These circumstances, however, made all the difference for human sympathy, empathy, and cognition. The development of empathy or the ability to suffer with another paid dividends in terms of fitness. Being able to feel the suffering of another allowed one to kill that person instead of being killed by that person. In addition empathy allowed greater internal cooperation among members of the ingroup. But the rise of these sorts of cognitive capacities also promoted the rise of conscious awareness, a development that changed everything. Killing became more difficult once killers understood that victims were just like the killers, that they had families, that they suffered, that they had hopes and dreams, and so forth. Thus in order to kill efficiently one had to develop forms of consciousness that allowed you to dissociate your Self from the act itself. Possession was one of these forms of consciousness. Of course possession states allow for much more than just the ability to kill with impunity and ferociousness, like a "berserker." Possession states also increase the ability to process information and to heal and so on. But killing and its ramifications were and are at the center of the possession experience.

Now consider the Otty Sanchez case from a theological point of view. How can a good God allow an innocent newborn to be tortured, torn apart, eaten, and killed by his own mother? What could possibly be more diabolical? Probably poor little Scotty awoke in the night crying seeking comfort, warmth, and food from his mother. Instead he received nothing but horror from her. Indeed why was Scotty brought into the world at all if all he got from it was a few weeks of chaotic care from a schizophrenic and depressed woman and then mutilation at her hands?

Can we muster any compassion at all for Otty Sanchez herself? She clearly has some awareness of the horror of what she did as she tried to kill herself. She will likely undergo treatment at the hands of doctors who will undoubtedly pull her out of her psychotic unawareness into a full awareness of her crime. Is that a good thing? It may only increase her pain and suffering.

Perhaps she will maintain through it all, her memory of how "she" did not really kill her baby—instead Satan did it as Satan had possessed her and she had lost control of her own will.

Why does Satan possess people? To do them harm. The standard Christian theological story concerning possession is that evil demons hate people because God loves us. Satan and his minions want to do us harm because they hate God. If God was not interested in us then neither would Satan be interested in us. Satan furthermore wants most of all to inflict suffering on the innocent as innocence is close to God—the closer to God you get, the greater a target you will become for Satan, or so the theological account goes.

Clearly this theologic account of the Otty Sanchez case does not easily square with the evolutionary account of infanticide or the medical account of psychosis. Not even the genetic conflict theory can fully account for these sorts of cases. In order to begin to understand adequately possession phenomena, particularly demonic possession, we will need a whole new theoretical approach that draws on evolutionary genetics, the brain sciences, anthropology, the cognitive sciences, and theology. One particularly important factor that I believes tips the balance of a possession experience into a negative or demonic experience is the intrusion of local group dynamics into the picture.

Depersonalization is the loss of individual awareness, autonomy, and self-control, and the transferral of basic functions of the self, such as empathy and intercourse with others, over to a group. In short there is a reduction in self-awareness and an increase in group or social identity. Typically the transfer of self is to a group that the individual identifies with. It is (to use a technical term) a highly entitative group. The group carries much of the individual's identity such that the individual is comfortable adopting the group's actions as his own. If the group stigmatizes some other out-group as noxious, so too will the individual, once deindividuation occurs. If the group acts with a kind of herd mentality, moving with fads or waves of irrational attachments to various salient "ideas," so too will the individual, once depersonalization occurs. If the group decides that violent elimination of other groups or of selected individuals is necessary, the individual member of the group will produce rationales to justify the violence, once depersonalization occurs.

I suggest that cases of negative possession involve a loss in the sense of agency and a transferral of the sense of self and control of self over to a group that can be characterized as an enterprise association—a group that imposes identities and "purposes" on its members. Thus, the individual's will is submerged in that of the group's purpose. Demonic possession therefore will always entail de-individuation of the possessed and an ongoing, group-controlled ritual display. In the case studies available to us the victim's relation to the local group is often not identified but in the many field studies of ecstatic spirit-possession cults published by anthropologists in the last century these group effects are clearly identified. The individual, as it were, "channels" group identities, forces, powers, and aims. In the course of human history these sorts of negative possession events typically occurred in two group contexts: women's fertility cults and aberrant or nonorthodox forms of religiosity. The latter often involved ingestion of hallucinogens that would then prevent control of the possession experience by the individual. This loss of control of the experience by the individual is the common denominator in all negative-possession phenomena. The loss of control left the individual at the mercy of predatory groups and deindividuation would ensue. It is important, however, to emphasize that demonic possession is not only a matter of deindividuation. Even in such extreme suffering as demonic possession the individual can still find a voice and can still communicate a message about her plight and about the groups she finds herself in. It is the duty of the scientists and clinicians who work with possession experiences to listen in a way that receives the message but does not endorse the method used to send the message. In order to hear the message sent by the victim and to understand the nature of the possession experience itself we need to approach the problem from as many angles as possible. I turn next to potential brain correlates of these negative possession experiences.

Chapter 2

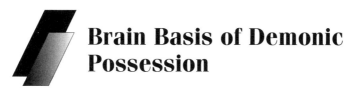

Brain Basis of Demonic Possession

To develop a naturalistic theory of the nature and functions of demonic possession it would help to understand its neuropsychologic correlates. Understanding the brain basis of possession might also lead to new somatic treatments for people who become possessed. The best way to study brain correlates of a demonic possession experience is to find someone who is currently possessed and then put that person through a neuroimaging protocol. To my knowledge this sort of study has not yet been done. There are no publications that I know of that describe functional magnetic resonance imaging scans or PET scans or computerized tomographic scans of brains of people who are demonically possessed. One can imagine how difficult it would be to do such a study. In lieu of direct brain scans of demonically possessed people we can begin to get a picture of the brain activity in a possessed person via systematic neuropsychologic investigation of the possessed and of people with disorders that are similar to possession states such as dissociative identity disorder and epilepsy. In addition, we can garner clues as to brain regions and functions implicated in possession by using the information we have addressed in other chapters on issues such as who gets possessed? What kind of behavioral and cognitive changes do the possessed undergo? And so on.

FACTS ABOUT POSSESSION THAT CAN YIELD CLUES AS TO ITS BRAIN CORRELATES

Who gets possessed? As we have seen, most scholars who have studied possession phenomena seem to believe that young women are more likely to undergo negative, demonic forms of possession than men or older women. I could, however, find no hard epidemiologic data on this issue.

I therefore conducted an informal analysis of all of the "complete" case studies available to me when writing this book.[1] Complete studies were defined as published cases that contained basic information on the possessed, the demon, behavioral changes in the possessed, and subsequent outcomes of the possession. There were 51 studies where enough information was presented on the case that that information could be scored unambiguously. We scored the sex and age of the possessed, the behaviors of the possessed, and the characteristics of the demon or demons who did the possessing. Here is what we found: females were far more likely to present with demonic possession than men (73% vs 27% respectively). A little over half (55%) of the cases involved adults; 20% involved young adults or teenagers. We were surprised to find that 12% of cases involved children. About half of the cases involved Christians. In the other half of the cases religion was unspecified. Virtually all of the cases (94%) contained descriptions of behavioral changes with 71% describing mental changes of one kind or another and a surprising 65% describing physical changes in the possessed. Here are some of the mental changes that were noted with demonic possession:

1. Personality/demeanor changed (e.g., affable person becomes quiet and isolative, a person begins to engage in hostile and/or paranoid thoughts);
2. Experienced apparent "onset" of multiple personalities and/or severe and abrupt mood changes;
3. Engaged in violent and/or abusive behavior (sometimes toward other humans/animals);
4. Appeared catatonic;
5. Insulted, cursed, and/or swore excessively (when that was uncharacteristic of that person's usual behavior);
6. Acted out sexually preoccupied thoughts (e.g., crudely sexual conversation, masturbating in front of others, etc.);
7. Participated in acts of humiliation (e.g., urinating on oneself);
8. Practiced self-mutilation;
9. Averse to religious objects (i.e., a person who normally went to church suddenly despised the thought, destroyed religious materials);
10. Experienced severe nightmares or night terrors;
11. Showed evidence of blackouts in memories;

---

[1] Actually, I did not conduct the data review and summary; my assistants did with my supervision. These able assistants were Emily Abrams, Andrea Avalos, and Michael Josephs.

12. Exhibited obvious changes in sleep patterns;
13. Lost or gain weight suddenly;
14. Changed dress;
15. Changed the way the person took care of himself (e.g., changes in personal hygiene);
16. Changed diet (foods that were once favorites were now repulsive and/or foods that were once detested were now favorites);
17. Exhibited "precognition" or the ability to predict the future;
18. Displayed "retro cognition" or the ability to know about past events that person should not know about;
19. Exhibited telepathic powers (knowing what someone else was thinking) or knew something about someone that person had not met; and
20. Exhibited clairvoyance or the ability to gain information about a person, location, or object through means other than the known human senses (e.g., feel what another person is feeling).

Often the physical changes involved changes in posture or strength or changes in the voice of the possessed—female voices became male voices, and so on. Here are some of the physical changes that could occur:

1. Spoke in tongues or a language they could not possibly know (or spoke with unusual accent);
2. Changed voice (e.g., high to low to guttural);
3. Became completely rigid so that he or she could be moved only with difficulty, even by multiple people;
4. Seemed to speak in multiple voices at the same time;
5. Did not blink eyes;
6. Changed eye or eye color (e.g., eyes turn black, almost like shark eyes);
7. Changed or distorted features in some way;
8. Possessed inhuman strength (e.g., multiple people had a difficult time restraining the possessed);
9. Moved in a way that seemed unusual and nonhuman-like (e.g., a person who seemed to glide instead of walk);
10. May have had writing or symbols on the body in the form of welts and scratches (especially in areas that the person could not physically reach);
11. May have had a decrease in body temperature although the surrounding room temperature stayed constant; and
12. Energy was drained; person had seemingly unexplainable fatigue.

Unusual occurrences were also very often noted—things like poundings on the floor or flying objects and the like. Here are some of these unusual occurrences:

1. Objects moved around seemingly by themselves (or objects flew around as if they were thrown from unseen hands);
2. Objects disappeared and could not be found again;
3. Objects disappeared (sometimes to be found in another location or later in same location, known as teleporting);
4. Knocking, banging or pounding could be heard in the surrounding environment (often heard in threes, as if mocking the Holy Trinity);
5. Religious articles disappeared or were destroyed;
6. Sounds (e.g., growling, howling, scratching, voices) could be heard and foul smells experienced, but the source could not be located;
7. Odd lights were seen or shot around a room;
8. People or dark shadows were seen that might or might not have form;
9. Sudden temperature fluctuations occurred (or temperature decreased);
10. There was a sensation of wind blowing even with the windows closed;
11. Doors and drawers opened and closed on their own;
12. Electrical appliances turned on or off seemingly by themselves;
13. Spontaneous fires started up;
14. Glass broke for no reason (or sounds of glass breaking were heard but there was no evidence of it happening);
15. Animals seemed to be frightened or bothered by something beyond human detection;
16. People had a feeling of being watched or that they were not alone;
17. Any talk of God or religion (or the recitation of prayers) caused an outbreak of activity;
18. Apparent retaliation took place after some attempt to stop the activity (i.e., consulting a clergyman, exorcism);
19. The possessed or others were attacked by a seemingly outside force (e.g., punching, scratching, biting, hair pulling, shoving to the ground);
20. The possessed was sexually assaulted by a seemingly outside force (e.g., fondling, penetration, rape);
21. Objects or people were levitated;

22. Involuntary babbling/cries/roars were heard that were obviously caused by an outside force; and
23. The possessed has involuntary movements/gestures that suggest possession by a spirit/demon; inhibition of normal functioning (e.g., seemingly unable to speak).

Demonic possession was far more common (73%) in this nonrepresentative sample of well-described cases than mere spirit possession (27%). Three-quarters of the cases (75%) involved possession by a single entity, but 24% involved possession by more than one entity. Most often the sex of the possessing spirit was unspecified but seemed to be male. In 39% of cases the possessing spirit was clearly male. In only 4% of cases was the possessing spirit clearly female. When cases were scored for the amount of aggression exhibited by the possessed the mean score was 5 out of a possible 8. Behavioral indices of "primitivity" included display of disinhibited or unsocialized impulses such as aggression and sexual impulses. Cases were scored a 3 out of a possible 5, indicating that many cases displayed extremely primitive impulsive behaviors. Two-thirds of our sample of possessed "patients" sought help, with one-half undergoing formal exorcism rituals; 82% of these exorcisms were successful but in one-third of the cases possession re-occurred after some interval of time.

Table 2.1
Victim demographics of possession case studies (N = 51)

Gender	Age	Religion
Male: 14 (27%)	Child: 6 (12%)	Catholic: 17 (33%)
Female: 37 (73%)	Teenage/young adult: 10 (20%)	Christian: 8 (16%)
	Adult: 28 (55%)	Jewish: 3 (6%)
	Elder: 3 (6%)	Unspecified: 23 (45%)
	Unspecified: 4 (7%)	

Table 2.2
Symptoms of possession

Any symptoms	48 of 51 (94%)
Mental	34 of 48 (71%)
Physical	31 of 48 (65%)
Outside force/occurrence	34 of 48 (71%)

Legend: See text for explanation.

Table 2.3
Demon information (N = 51)

What is possessing the victim?	Demons/spirits	
	Number	Gender
Demon: 34 (73%)	One: 38 (75%)	Male: 20 (39%)
Spirit: 14 (27%)	More than one: 12 (24%)	Female: 2 (4%)
Other: 2 (4%)	Unspecified: 1 (2%)	Unspecified: 29 (57%)
Unspecified 1 (2%)		
Primitivity Scale:	Mean: 3.09	Mode: 3
Aggression Scale:	Mean: 5.00	Mode: 7

Table 2.4
Treatment information

Deliberately sought treatment	29 of 44 (66%)
Consulted someone to help	27 of 42 (64%)
Exorcism performed	22 of 42 (52%)
Possession stopped after exorcism	18 of 22 (82%)
Repossession occurred	6 of 18 (33%)

What does this cursory analysis of 51 well-described cases tell us about demonic possession? Results of the analysis are consistent with our discussion of case studies and with the views of authorities who have written on the topic. If we perhaps unwisely treat this small set of cases as representative of the general population of people who become possessed, then we would have to conclude that females are more likely to become demonically possessed than males, and that the possessing demonic agent is almost always male or unspecified but very rarely female, and that behavior of the possessed is very disinhibited, involving display of unsocialized sexual and aggressive impulses. Exorcism rituals furthermore are extremely effective in curing patients of this affliction. One-third of patients, however, experience a relapse or recurrence of the "illness." In most cases there are also all kinds of "paranormal" manifestations as well—at least this is what observers report. These paranormal phenomena are fascinating as many involve unusual feats or capacities of mental life or cognitive processing. Of course, extreme caution is in order when interpreting this set of data. These 51 cases are *not* a random sampling of all of the cases of demonic possession that have ever occurred. Generalizations based on this sample therefore must be cautious. It would be more accurate to characterize this sample along the following lines:

> These are a small sampling of cases that made it into the published record and that McNamara was able to find and deem "well-described" after relatively intensive searches in books and journals available to a large urban university in 2008–2009.

On the other hand this sample's characteristics are congruent with estimations and statements of most other scholars who have studied possession phenomena over the last couple of centuries. Negative forms of possession tend to involve women being possessed by male demons and engaging in profoundly disinhibited aggressive and sexual displays. It is these kinds of facts that have led many scholars to claim that negative possessions, and "ecstatic states" more generally, are used by women the world over as a political tool to turn the tables on oppressive patriarchal groups and institutional structures. Whatever the functional uses of negative possession for women, it seems to me that we must conclude that these facts are relatively accurate . . . demonic forms of possession occur mostly in women and involve possession by a male demon that displays antisocial and antireligious behaviors. Even if this later turns out to be false as a characterization of the entire population of cases involving demonic possession, it *must* be the case that a significant portion of cases of demonic possession involves females and male demons. So even if we cannot claim that we are piecing together the phenomenology of all cases of demonic possession, we can safely claim that we are building on a significant portion of the possession dataset, namely that portion of the dataset involving females who become possessed. So what might be the brain correlates of demonic possession involving females who are possessed by male demonic agents?

THE FEMALE BRAIN DIFFERS ON AVERAGE FROM THE MALE BRAIN

Not surprisingly, the brains of females differ in significant ways from the brains of males. Sex differences in the brain are largely determined by steroid hormone exposure during a perinatal sensitive period that alters subsequent behaviors throughout the lifespan. There have now been hundreds of studies on sex differences in the human brain but there is as of yet no strong consensus on what those studies demonstrate. I think it is fair to say that when one controls for overall brain volume, women have a higher percentage of gray matter and men a higher percentage of white matter with structures in the left hemisphere being slightly larger in woman than in men (Cosgrove, Mazure, and Staley 2007). Women may also represent language functions in both hemispheres while men's representation of language functions is primarily left-sided. Women are more vulnerable to aphasic and other language disorders no matter what hemisphere sustains a stroke while men tend to get aphasia with left-hemisphere strokes only.

Brun et al. (2009) applied a new method to compare the three-dimensional profile of sex differences in brain structure based on MRI scans of 50 men with 50 women, matched for age and other relevant demographics. They found that left-hemisphere auditory and language-related regions were proportionally larger in women versus men. In men, primary visual and visuo-spatial association areas of the parietal lobes were proportionally expanded. These results are consistent with the better performance by women versus men on verbal tasks and the better performance of men versus women on spatial tasks.

All of these aforementioned findings suggests that functional *cognitive* differences in men and women become manifest primarily at the hemispheric level. Interestingly, functional cerebral asymmetries are, in fact, sex specific: While they are relatively stable in men, they are reduced during the menstrual cycle in women, indicating that sex hormones might play an important role in modulating interhemispheric communication and functioning brain (Weis and Hausmann 2010).

In an important respect, then, women appear to be less functionally lateralized than men. Women's bilateral representation of language-related functions and more fluid interhemispheric communication gives them an advantage over men in language-dependent forms of information processing. On the other hand, women pay a price for this reduced (relative to men) asymmetry in that they are deficient relevant to men in spatially based forms of information processing. This latter functional difference is seen clearly in the case of Turner's syndrome.

Turner's syndrome (TS) individuals lack the male Y chromosome and are phenotypically female. TS behavioral features can be associated not only with complete monosomy X but also with partial deletions of either the short (Xp) or long (Xq) arm of the X chromosome (partial monosomy X). TS individuals are typically impaired on visual-spatial/perceptual tasks but are intact on language-processing tasks. The lack of the male chromosome leads to androgen deficiency during development of the neuraxis and thus the brain does not masculinize during development (Ross, Roeltgen, and Zinn 2006).

Thus, both XX females and TS individuals outperform males on verbal tasks, and both demonstrate behavioral signs of reduced asymmetry in terms of brain organization. Interestingly, homosexual men also tend to outperform heterosexual men on verbal tasks. Indeed their performance profiles on cognitive tasks tend to be more like females than males (see Collaer, Reimers, and Manning 2007). Homosexuals are known to have a higher frequency of atypical lateralization for some functional traits, such as handedness (Lalumière, Blanchard, and Zucker 2000).

Taken together these data from adult females, TS females, and male homosexuals suggests that the feminized brain is characterized by a reduction in the asymmetrical organization that characterizes the brain of heterosexual adult males. What is the relevance of all this to demonic possession phenomena? As we have seen above females are more likely to become possessed than males. I now want to suggest that those males that are more vulnerable to possession are males with reductions in cerebral asymmetry that are like the reductions seen in the female and homosexual brains. In short, a reduction in asymmetry may be a risk factor for demonic possession.

A reduction in asymmetry, however, is not all that is required for possession. Older people evidence reductions in cerebral asymmetry and they are not as likely to become demonically possessed as younger females. On the other hand, older people in traditional societies are much more likely to become spirit possessed (positive spirit possession) and experience religious visions (see the narratives in Walker 1991). Perhaps it is a matter of degree. The young female brain may be more "symmetric" or less lateralized than the older individual's brain, which is more symmetric relative to the young adult heterosexual male. At present we cannot decide this issue. It may be as well that a particular form of reduction in asymmetry is necessary to enhance the odds of possession. After all, many brain disorders involve reductions in the typical asymmetric organization of brain functions among other brain changes. While most of these disorders do involve changes in religiosity, they do not always or even frequently lead to possession. Nevertheless they can be associated with possession. Consider the case of epilepsy. Epilepsy involves brain tissue, usually deep in the temporal lobes, that is somehow damaged and around which develop groups of neurons that discharge in synchronous fashion. The synchronous firing of groups of neurons is associated with seizures. It has long been noted that one form of epilepsy, temporal-lobe epilepsy (TLE), can occasionally be associated with heightened religiosity. Patients describe intense religious experiences or undergo repeated conversions to different religious sects or ideologies and so on. Trimble and Freeman (2006) looked at the clinical correlates of TLE patients with and without self-reported high interest in religion and compared these two groups of patients to a healthy control group of regular churchgoers. They found that the hyperreligious TLE patients more frequently had bilateral seizure foci than unilateral (right or left) foci and more frequently reported episodes of post-ictal psychoses. Compared to the healthy churchgoer group, hyperreligious TLE patients more often reported actual experiences of some great spiritual figure or supernatural being—either an evil presence or a benign spiritual presence.

If we can associate bilateral seizure foci with reduced asymmetry, then the epilepsy data can be read as partially consistent with the idea that reduced asymmetry increases risk for spirit-possession phenomena. Just how does reduced asymmetry, especially in the case of epilepsy, give rise to heightened religiosity and possession phenomena? With respect to the issue of heightened religiosity, Geschwind (1979) argued that that symptom was often associated with hypergraphia (a tendency to highly detailed writing often of a religious or philosophical nature), hyposexuality (diminished sex drive), and irritability of varying degree. In TLE over-excitation or hyperconnectivity between limbic and temporal sites leads to the TLE behaviors where everything but sex is significant and requires attention. That sense of heightened significance gives rise to religiosity. What causes the hyperconnectivity? If interhemispheric callosal fibers can no longer inhibit their targets in the opposite hemisphere, then the reduction in transcallosal inhibition will lead to enhanced bilateral subcortical to cortical functional connectivity.

Bear and Fedio (1977), in fact, argued that heightened religiosity was due to a greater number or density of connections between cortical sites handling the senses and the limbic system, including the amygdala, so that patients with TLE experienced a greater number of sensory events as "significant" relative to a healthy person with fewer such connections. In their recent review of religious and spiritual experiences in epilepsy Devinsky and Lai (2008) largely endorse the hyperconnection model for interictal hyperreligiosity and they agree with Trimble and Freeman that interictal religiosity may be linked with bilateral temporal-lobe seizure foci. But can possession phenomena emerge from the reduction in asymmetry associated with epilepsy?

Now consider the following cases reported by Carrazana et al. (1999).

Case 1

This 24-year-old Haitian man had his first generalized tonic-clonic seizure at the age of 17 years during the wake of an uncle. The patient had been sleep deprived during the vigil of the corpse. The seizure was attributed to possession by Ogu (the warrior god), the dead uncle's protecting loa. Subsequent seizures and morning myoclonus were explained as harassment by the wandering soul of the uncle. The possession was interpreted as a punishment, for the patient had been disrespectful toward the deceased in the past. He was treated by the local mambo (priest) for 6 years and did not see a physician until coming to the United States. His EEG showed 3- to 4-Hz bursts of generalized spike-wave complex discharges occurring spontaneously and during photic stimulation. In retrospect, the patient had a history of waking myoclonus, which had been ignored. He remained seizure free after treatment with valproic acid (VPA). The likely diagnosis is juvenile myoclonic epilepsy. (Carrazana et al. 1999,239)

Comment: This case does not tell us anything specific about reduced asymmetry as a contributing cause to the possession. But the sleep disorder is interesting as it may have involved a form of reduced asymmetry manifesting as a parasomnia. Both seizure and sleep disorders promote parasomnias or difficulty transitioning from one sleep state into another or from sleep to waking. Dissociative identity disorder (DID) can also be understood as involving difficulty in keeping brain states appropriately separated from one another and DID can involve possession phenomena. But let us continue with the issue of epilepsy and possession.

Case 2

This 27-year-old Haitian woman, with a history of complex partial and secondarily generalized seizures since adolescence, was the product of a long and difficult delivery, which was attributed to a "grip" in the mother's belly by a loa. At the age of 14 years, she fell in an open fire during a seizure and suffered extensive burns to her arm, leg, and parts of the face and trunk. Burns were treated at a local hospital, but the family brought the patient back to the mambo to treat the "possession." This incident was interpreted by the mambo as possession by "Marinnette." Marinnette-bwa-chech is one of the most dreaded loas, an agent for underhand dealings and an expert sorceress. Those possessed by this loa are said to throw themselves in the fire and stamp about until they put the flames out. The patient had bitemporal independent spikes on EEG. Treatment with antiepileptic drugs (AEDs) has decreased the frequency of seizures. (Carrazana et al. 1999,239–240)

Comment: The possession experience in this case was associated with bitemporal spikes, thus implying reduced asymmetry.

Case 3

This 36-year-old woman had several years of recurrent complex partial seizures that manifested as a strong sense of fear and epigastric coldness, followed by loss of awareness, utterances of nonsensical phrases, and complex motor automatisms. The local mambo attributed the events to her being taken by "Melle Charlotte," a french loa, with the nonsensical speech being interpreted as a foreign language. It is said that during the possession by this spirit, a person will speak perfect French or other languages, even though in life, the person has no knowledge of that language. She continued to have seizures despite the mambo's attempts to conjure the spirit. He explained his failure to the fact that Melle Charlotte is a very particular loa who makes only sporadic appearances. She was not treated with AEDs until she left Haiti at the age of 34. An EEG revealed a right anterior temporal focus, and magnetic resonance imaging (MRI) showed right hippocampal atrophy. Seizures improved with carbamazepine (CBZ), although compliance with medication was a problem, largely because of family interference. (Carrazana et al. 1999,240)

Comment: This case is particularly interesting as glossolalia was part of the clinical picture. Also we have localizing information: the EEG revealed a right anterior temporal focus. This is a site implicated in hyperreligosity (see McNamara 2009).

Case 4

This 44-year-old Dominican woman (of Haitian parents) for years has been experiencing partial seizures which she refers to as "la cosa" (the thing). Her seizures, with a sudden overwhelming sensation of emptiness, were attributed to her "good angel" leaving her as the spirit of the dead tried to take hold of her ("me mandaron un muerto"). The sending of the dead, l 'envs morts, is a feared Voodoo curse, which is said to affect health and prosperity. The mambo explained the failure of the attacks to respond to his exorcisms to the strong hold of the spirit. EEG showed a right temporal focus, and the MRI was normal. Seizures were controlled with phenytoin (PHT) monotherapy. (Carrazana et al. 1999, 240)

Comment: Once again we have localizing information that refers to right temporal lobes as the site of the focus. In addition, in this case the patient was able to report an experience associated with the switch in identities. She felt an emptying out before the onset of the negative possession experience.

Case 5

This 47-year-old Jamaican woman of Haitian descent, with a history of Chiari I malformation, syringomyelia, and arrested hydrocephalus, has a long-standing history of complex partial seizures with and without secondary generalization. The patient and her family attributed the seizures to Voodoo spirit possessions, being influenced by the olfactory hallucination of a burning smell, and a rising epigastric aura "taking over the body." A prolonged postictal psychosis would follow, in which the patient would alternate chanting and wooing with periods of total unresponsiveness. EEG demonstrated independent bitemporal interictal epileptiform discharges. She denied her diagnosis of epilepsy, resisted diagnostic and therapeutic interventions, and insisted that she was possessed by spirits of the dead. On immigrating to the United States, she ultimately became seizure free with PHT monotherapy. (Carrazana et al. 1999, 240)

Comment: Bitemporal foci and reduced asymmetry appear to be associated with more severe phenomenology than cases with right-sided foci. It is striking how convinced the patient apparently was that she was possessed by spirits of the dead. We are not told by Carrazana et al. if treatment with antiseizure medicine also treated the delusional beliefs (assuming that the beliefs were delusional).

These cases of negative possession states from Carrazana et al. (1999) are interesting for development of a neurology of possession because where localizing information was available it implicated either reduced asymmetry in the form of bitemporal foci or the anterior temporal lobe on the right side.

DID AND POSSESSION

Dissociative identity disorder (DID; previously known as multiple personality disorder) is the most severe and chronic manifestation of the more fundamental cognitive capacity to dissociate one's identity from trauma or memory of trauma. There is a continuum of capacity to enter into and "use" dissociative states for various culturally sanctioned uses (Seligman and Kirmayer 2008). I will review the ability to enter dissociative states for positive cultural functions below. Although everyone appears to have the capacity to enter dissociative mind states, occasionally the process goes awry, resulting in mental disorder.

Dysfunctional dissociation can manifest as the presence of two or more distinct identities or personality states that recurrently take control of the individual's behavior. There may be transient amnesia or fugue states and in extreme cases changes in neuropsychologic performance that, in turn, point to dynamic changes in brain organization associated with the dissociative process. Is there evidence for reduced asymmetry in DID? Most authorities suggest that while dissociation is common in both men and women, DID is more common among women. In addition, non-right-handedness appears to be more common in DID than in the general population. Indeed there are cases where handedness switched with a switch in identities states (Savitz et al. 2004). As we have seen above, reduced asymmetry is associated with non-right-handedness. Non-right-handedness, in turn, can be associated with unusual cognitive and behavioral phenomena such as mirror writing in which the individual writes in a script that is a mirror reflection of typical right-handed scripts. Mirror writing must require bilateral communication between the motor engrams for script in each hemisphere (i.e., a reduction in asymmetry). Thus, if DID is associated with reduced asymmetry we should see cases of mirror writing in DID patients. Le, Smith, and Cohen (2009) in fact report just such a case.

There are very few studies of neuroimaging of patients with DID. One such study reported significantly smaller volumes of the hippocampus and amygdala among those with DID as compared to healthy controls (Vermetten et al. 2006; though see Smeets, Jelicic, and Merckelbach, 2006). An fMRI study of a woman diagnosed with co-morbid DID and PTSD (Tsai et al. 1999) reported that the switch from native to alter personality involved bilateral hippocampal inhibition, thus indicating reduced asymmetry. The right parahippocampal and medial temporal regions were also inhibited. Finally there was inhibition of small regions of the globus pallidus and substantia nigra. Interestingly, switching back to the native personality was associated with activation of the *right-sided hippocampus*. This latter result implies that re-establishment of normal asymmetric brain organization is associated with normalization of ego-identity states.

In summary, DID patients fit the profile of reduced asymmetry—they tend to be female and non-right-handed. In behavioral experiments using dichotic listening paradigms individuals high on dissociative experiences scales, evidence reduced asymmetry (Marinos 1997). With respect to the mechanics of the switch to an alter personality, there is a reduction in asymmetry via inhibition of structures in both hemispheres. For DID that inhibition involves hippocampal functions. Given that the hippocampus is involved in memory consolidation it seems reasonable to suppose that hippocampal inhibition in DID mediates DID associated amnesia.

Taken together with the evidence from TLE and the DID, data suggest that possession may involve an inability to activate right-sided hippocampal and amygdalar structures in order to support ongoing ego-identity functions. Instead, asymmetry of organization and function is blocked and the individual operates out of an altered identity.

ALTERED STATES OF CONSCIOUSNESS AND POSSESSION

Dissociative ability has been proposed as a universal trait or capacity that lies along a continuum that measures the ability to enter altered states of consciousness. All people possess the trait to some degree and people with DID lie at one extreme of the continuum. As we have seen dissociative ability may act as a diathesis that when trauma is present may push the individual toward full-blown DID. DID patients are thought to be highly hypnotizable and to exhibit other phenomena such as absorption, high imagery or fantasy preference, frequent mystical or spiritual experiences, time distortions, and so on, collectively called "altered states of consciousness" or ASC. Given the wide diversity and phenomenology of ASC it seems unlikely that there will be any single neurologic account of the experiences. Yet I would like to suggest that reduced asymmetry plays a critical role in all ASC. Reduced asymmetry cannot account for all manifestations or symptoms of ASC but I suggest that reduced asymmetry is one crucial anatomical common denominator for increasing the frequency and intensity of ASC.

Smith (2008) showed that absorption, as measured by the Tellegen Absorption Scale (TAS) was a significant predictor of intensity and frequency of mystical experiences. Laidlaw et al. (2005) showed that individuals with low "self-directedness" (SD) scores on the temperament and character inventory (perhaps indicating relatively weak central ego-identity functions) proved to have significantly raised scores on hypnotizability, absorption, self-transcendence, and significantly lower scores on co-operativeness. Prohaska (2002) compared the *trait absorption* scores as measured by the Tellegen Absorption Scale (TAS), and religious orientation as measured by the Religious Orientation Scale (ROS) among 261 adults between ages 25 and 78 (M = 46.7) who verbally reported no serious mental disorder or physical disease. She found elevated absorption capacities among the intrinsically oriented versus the extrinsically oriented religious responders. The intrinsically religious participants had 21% higher absorption scores than the extrinsically religious participants or nonreligious participants. Interestingly Spanos et al. (1980) found that absorption predicted dream recall rates in females but not males. Finkel and McGue (1997) applied a behavior genetic model including sex limitation of heritability to personality data from 1,257 twin families. Data indicated lower female heritability for alienation and control and higher female heritability for absorption. The gene that codes for the enzyme catechol-O-methyltransferase (COMT, which is involved in cortical dopamine catabolism), and a serotoninergic receptor gene have been linked to trait absorption. Ott et al. (2005) reported a significant interaction effect between the 5-HT2a and the COMT genes such that hypnotic absorption scores were highest in subjects homozygous for the TT-genotype of 5-HT2a as well as for the VAL/VAL genotype of COMT. Given that the trait absorption/hypnotic susceptibility is correlated with measures of religiousness (Batson, Shoenrade, and Ventis 1993, 112–113) and dissociative abilities, it seems likely that these genes have influenced variation in levels of dissociative abilities and religiosity across individuals.

Vaitl et al. (2005) conducted an exhaustive review of the literature on the psychobiology of ASC and reported that ASC can be characterized in terms of alteration in each of four psychobiologic dimensions: activation, awareness span, self-awareness, and sensory dynamics. Crossing these four dimensions with the source of induction into the ASC, results in a relatively complete phenomenology of existing ASC. Contrary, however, to Vaitl et al.'s classification of hypnotic phenomena, I would classify hypnosis (the ASC closest to the trait dissociation and absorption that we have been considering here) as high on activation and arousal, but low on self-awareness and a constricted awareness span, depending partially on induction method (self versus environmentally induced by a hypnotist). Absorption clearly involves a restriction of awareness span to one or a small set of objects or events along with a transient reduction in sense of self. All of these cognitive alterations allow for extraordinary forms of information processing and unusual experiential phenomena, including the capacity to experience possession.

How, then, might absorption work physiologically? Consistent with the flow of the argument in this chapter I suggest that reduced asymmetry is the key to absorption and related phenomena. Many investigators (see Dietrich 2004 for a recent review) have suggested that prefrontal inhibition and limbic disinhibition are the key neurodynamic correlates of "flow" or of absorption and related states. Nakamura and Csikszent-mihalyi (2005) suggest that flow is a state of complete absorption attained during activities whose perceived challenges precisely match the subject's skill level so that attention is effortlessly engaged, directed, and maintained. The experience is usually quite enjoyable. Flow likely involves a transient inhibition of midline callosal structures supporting self/agency and then a heightened integration across hemispheres of subcortical basal ganglia and limbic systems with prefrontal attentional and self-regulatory systems. In short, flow and absorption likely involve a transient reduction in asymmetrical brain organization in order to facilitate integrative capacities of both hemispheres. This is the crux of the matter with respect to possession states. Both negative and positive possession states can involve enhanced cognitive capacities. These are transient in the case of negative possession and enduring in the case of positive possession. Reduced asymmetry likely always involves both costs and benefits when it comes to information processing. Everything depends on whether the initial reduction in transcallosal inhibition is followed by a process or phase of limbic-cortical integration. In positive possession this is the case, but in negative possession the integrative process occurs for some while but eventually breaks down entirely and then the negative possession is merely destructive. During that transient period when some integrative processing is still occurring we see those striking manifestations of demonic possession when the "devil" demonstrates paranormal knowledge of foreign or ancient languages or precognitive or clairvoyant sight and so on.

Only future research will clarify the issues of brain correlates of demonic possession experiences. But if we keep in mind the available neuropsychologic data and how it points to a consistent reduction in asymmetry as a predictor for dissociative states and possession, then it becomes less surprising that pharmacologic agents have long been used to induce possession. Virtually all known hallucinogenic agents alter the interhemispheric interaction patterns. For example, Serafetinides (1965) in the 1960s showed that LSD had no effects in patients whose right temporal lobes had been removed. All hallucinogenic agents appear to induce their effects by altering serotoninergic and dopaminergic activity levels in right-sided temporal and prefrontal sites. By doing so these pharmacologic agents reduce the normal asymmetry that these neurotransmitter systems normally support. Since the era of the Upper Paleolithic some 50,000 years ago and very likely even before that, human beings have been taking psychoactive substances to induce altered states of consciousness and more specifically spirit-possession experiences. People did not ingest these substances merely to become deranged. They took these "entheogens" to experience the supernatural. The drugs had specific effects on the brain, not global effects. Those specific effects must have involved some reduction in the normal pattern of asymmetry by heightening the activity of one hemisphere over the other.

Chapter 3

Freud's Treatment of Religion and Demonic Possession

Sigmund Freud produced one of the most profound set of meditations on the origins and functions of religion ever published, yet his work is all too often dismissed by religion scholars as fanciful and derogatory toward religion. It is easy to see why critics thought he was hostile to religion. In interviews with the press and certainly in his books he often called it infantile and a delusion. On the other hand, in his major works on religion he displays an appreciation for the civilizational accomplishments of religion. He argues at length that religion allowed human beings to handle deeply aggressive and conflicting impulses in a constructive manner. Indeed he seems to argue that religion made cooperation within and between human groups possible. He then presents a theory as to how religion accomplished this feat. In the development of his theory of religion he also had occasion to examine a case of demonic possession. I will discuss that case and Freud's analysis of it below, but first I wish to present some of Freud's theories concerning religion's origins and functions as they can be read in terms of the contributions of spirit possession to the origins of religion. Freud, of course, does not argue as I do that spirit possession made religion possible but he does give us a detailed discussion of possible cognitive and emotional dynamics that made spirit possession possible for our ancestors and for us today. There are some crucial differences between my own views and Freud's and I will highlight them below but I still feel that Freud can be read profitably for insights into the biopsychological foundations of religion.

Both Freud and I see religious experiences as arising in part from conflicts both within an individual and between an individual (who identifies with one group) and some outgroup. Freud's distinct contribution in my view lies in his insistence that guilt is crucial for religious experience. This is a great insight and one consistent with centuries of theological specula- tion concerning the religious condition of humankind. But Freud's analy- sis of guilt, I will argue, is incomplete. He sees it as arising essentially from the primeval oedipal conflict (more on this below). While I agree that something like a primeval oedipal conflict is operative in triggering guilt among other emotions, the oedipal conflict and related biopsycho- logic mechanisms do not exhaust the phenomenon of guilt. Freud con- nects guilt with the phenomena of asceticism and of sacrifice. Certainly sacrifice—bloody sacrifice—is at the heart of the religious consciousness so Freud was on the right track in that regard. Again, however, I will argue that Freud missed the most important aspects of guilt that can explain reli- gious phenomena, but at least he realized (along with all the great theolo- gians in the monotheistic religions) that guilt and sacrifice were key to the religious mystery.

So what did Freud miss when he considered guilt? In my view Freud is correct in arguing that guilt is at the center of religious experience, but the reason it is so central is that it requires self-awareness and self-reflection to operate. Although guilt may have evolved in the first place to facilitate pro-social social interactions such as within-group cooperation, it had the secondary consequence of dramatically increasing self-reflective thought and self-awareness in those individuals capable of feeling guilt. In fact guilt both produces and requires an awareness of a current self (who I am now) and an awareness of a counterfactual or a potential future self (who I should have been or who I should become) as well as a computational estimate of the discrepancy between the current and counterfactual selves to operate. Guilt is a motivational system that uses self-awareness as its fuel. Most important, it yields an experience of the dignity of personhood. Guilt can only be triggered when there is an offense against something that is reverenced. While crimes and insults against others can and should occasion guilt, the ultimate source of guilt is what these offenses do to the self and its dignity. It is this dignity of the self—the conscious, reflective self—that is at the heart of the religious experience. Without it no posses- sion states would be possible and no guilt would be possible and no sac- rifice and no religion. But the dignity of the reflective self can be offended and this incurs guilt if the offense is self inflicted and compassion and pity for the other if the offense is committed by another. Once one has experi- enced this sort of conscious awareness of the infinite worth of the self, one can only feel pity for those who do not know the experience. In addition, once one has the experience, all other values are relativized in relation to the experience. Guilt is the attempt to run away from that experience and Freud understood that fact intuitively. Let us now follow Freud in his reflections on the origins of guilt, religion, and the negative possession experience.

FREUD'S THEORIES OF RELIGION

Freud apparently grappled with the problem of religion all his life and thus his assessment of religion and religion's functions changed over time. His major works on religion were *Totem and Taboo* (1913), *The Future of an Illusion* (1927), *Civilization and Its Discontents* (1930), and *Moses and Monotheism* (1938). I am interested only in selective sections of some of these works. In *Totem and Taboo* Freud argues that sacrificial religion has its origins in a dim memory of an ancient murder of a father or an alpha male who enjoyed exclusive access to females. Males who were left out of that access (they were conceived as kin or even brothers) of course wanted to get access to females so they formed an alliance among themselves and then killed the father. While this sounds fanciful, it is actually not that far-fetched. This sort of scenario would not be too surprising to scientists familiar with the many nonhuman primate societies that are organized hierarchically around an alpha male who monopolizes access to fertile females at the expense (in terms of reproductive fitness) of all other males in the troupe. These primate societies depended on this social organization in order to survive. The alpha male, for example, could prevent infanticide by competitor males and could prevent violence and rape against females in his harem and so forth. The mere presence of the alpha male could inhibit violence of all kinds in the troupe. Crossing the alpha male was a fearsome prospect as he would intimidate and violently oppose any challenge to his authority. His presence commanded fear and respect. Thus members of the troupe had a lot invested in the alpha male. His demise could spell chaos and violence for everyone in the troupe.

We are descended from these primates and it is part of our genetic heritage. Freud was right to infer that creating a coalition of nondominant males to take on the alpha male must have been a fearsome prospect for those males. They had to brave death, injury, and the very dissolution of the old group ways if they were going to get access to females. To solidify the coalition they must have relied on kinship ties and if that was not possible (since most young males came from outside the group), then some form of reciprocal altruism must have been tried. In any case, once the coalition was formed, the attack on the alpha male became inevitable. Primatologists have documented many instances where coalitions of nondominant males take on a reigning alpha male. Blood is always shed, infanticide is usually part of the picture, and order is only restored with great battles among the usurpers and with great difficulty by a new alpha male. This sort of group organization—though it persists today among several primate societies—was not ideal. Thus, innovations were necessary in primate group social structure. Those innovations in social structure were accomplished in the line of primates that led to us. We nevertheless surely retain some of the "old ways" in our genes and brains.

It is important to point out that the issue of access to females by nondominant males may have become an increasingly urgent problem in the evolutionary line leading to us as brains of infants began to enlarge in that evolutionary pathway. As infants began to require more calories (to support those larger brains), females needed help getting those calories to their infants. That help was found in two places: the maternal grandmother of the child and nondominant males seeking access to the fertile female. Detailed modeling studies show that both sources of help were needed to bring a *Homo erectus* infant to maturity. Thus, both the females and the nondominant males had an interest in getting rid of the alpha-male social organization of traditional primate society. Coalitions of nondominant males may have received tacit help from the females in dethroning the alpha male. But in doing so they needed to find a way to prevent the violence and infanticide that usually followed the dethronement of the alpha male. Concealed ovulation, pair-bonding (to reduce paternity uncertainty), and female coalitions (that may have involved synchronized ovulatory cycles) all worked to neutralize male violence against females and their children.

Now what Freud contributes to this picture of attack on the alpha male is something very interesting. He suggests that when the nondominant males killed the alpha male, it was done with ambivalence, given the risks involved, and that ambivalence eventuated (for anatomically modern humans) in the social emotion we call guilt. At the level of the individual psyche, Freud would argue, guilt arises in the desire to kill the father so as to have exclusive access to the mother, that is, the oedipal complex.

The alpha-male/father is a block to reproductive fitness for young males in the troupe. Within an individual psyche of a young boy the father represents a block or a "No!" to the son who wants to monopolize the attention and resources of the mother. The paternal prohibition on monopolization of maternal attention, Freud argues, is one of the background emotional contexts for development of a young boy's ability to delay gratification of impulses more generally. This is a very important point for the theory of religion. All religions teach that morality is dependent on the ability to inhibit selfish impulses. From a neuroeconomic point of view religion allows us to avoid extreme temporal discounting curves—to favor current pleasures over future rewards. Behavioral economists who study temporal discounting phenomena (the tendency to prefer smaller rewards *now* in lieu of larger rewards later) posit a conflict between two selves within the individual: a current self who wants the reward now and a future self who wants to receive the rewards when he becomes real, that is, in the future. Both Freud and the economists understand that this conflict between immediate gratification and delayed gratification is absolutely fundamental to human behavior and society. Without the ability to deny current pleasures in favor of future rewards, no future savings would be possible and thus no accumulation of financial or cultural capital would be possible. All of civilization is built upon this fundamental cognitive ability to inhibit current gratification of desires in order to obtain greater rewards in the future.

The behavioral economists, however, treat the whole matter in abstraction from the real emotional context in which this ability is learned. Freud reminds us that the father is the one who usually teaches his children how to say no to immediate gratification of impulses. This situation sets up a cauldron of emotional conflict within the child during development. We need to pay attention to this developmental emotional cauldron if we want to understand this fundamental ability of inhibition of impulsivity. Ultimately, religion is brought in to handle the problem but that is getting ahead of our story. Let us return to our guide in these matters: Freud.

Freud tells us that the ability to delay gratification of impulses is not only inextricably linked to the developmental life of children but it is embedded in what he calls the oedipal complex. The father's ability to block the young boy's monopolization of the mother's attention and resources brings the boy face to face with the reality principle. That paternal "No!," however, only works if the young boy can learn to inhibit his desires and impulses. The young boy apparently needs to do this learning by navigating through a morass or cauldron of emotions of longing for the mother and of ambivalence, fear, reverence, anger, hatred, and ultimately guilt toward the father, with guilt being primary. Why guilt? No attempt will be made to inhibit impulses unless there is an outside force that commands it (Father) and then a growing inside awareness that that inhibition is necessary though difficult to attain (guilt). Paradoxically, then, guilt arises when the boy incorporates the paternal injunction and gives up the mother (kills the mother, not the father). The focus on young boys in all of this is absolutely crucial because in most primate societies and in human societies young unattached males will wreak havoc on the group unless they are given access to females or are controlled by some powerful force.

So one source of guilt is the failure to inhibit desires for short-term rewards and that sort of guilt is linked to the paternal prohibition and depends on awareness that there is a future that needs to be thought about and planned for. Thus, the desire to kill the father implies the elimination of the ability to inhibit current impulses, or the disregard for future selves or future plans. To choose to be the slave of current impulses is an affront to dignity but only if one is aware of the emotion we call dignity. Only individuals with dignity command the respect of others. People respect self-command, foresight, and so forth. An individual who could plan for the future was an invaluable asset to early humans. Such individuals could outfox competitors, could track and capture big prey, and could even predict the weather. They must have seemed like gods to early humans. When a boy was inclined to refuse to learn to eschew gratification of desires in favor of a dignified self, guilt might serve as a prompt to do better.

But how does guilt fit into Freud's theory of religion and into the larger story of spirit possession? Freud suggests that the origin of guilt was not, as I contend, a failure to become a dignified self; instead, that failure to delay gratification of immediate impulse led to murder, specifically murder of the father, and murderous impulses and acts lead to guilt. Human beings don't just fail to become "persons" with inherent dignity, they sink to the level of murderers. The memory of the original "murder" of the alpha-male father by a coalition of nondominant males (and perhaps females) created a sense of chronic, unrelenting guilt, according to Freud. The guilt is felt afresh in each boy's life as he sees the father as a competitor for the mother's attentions. The boy's fresh guilt is combined with the collective memory of the original murder to produce an overwhelming sense of guilt. This chronic sense of guilt had to be handled somehow by the psychic apparatus. One way to handle the guilt, according to Freud, was to enshrine the father image as God. He explains this psychic transformation of guilt into a religion in detail in *Totem and Taboo*, using as primary sources anthropological writings of his time. Freud views core aspects of religiousness as defense mechanisms against this murder, similar to the latency period in an individual's development. During the latency period, the child wants to murder the father in order to monopolize the mother's attentions and then feels guilty for this desire. To defend against this guilt the child builds a superego that incorporates the father's injunctions against gratification of impulses. On a theological level the concept of "original sin" becomes "thinkable" in order to explain the chronic sense of culpability that each individual carries within himself for having entertained murderous impulses against the father.

Freud was right to link guilt with transgression and taboo. Taboo in pre-modern societies was a kind of precursor to the purity regulations of more complex societies, including many of the world religions that persist and flourish to this day. Purity regulations in turn are linked to the sacred kingship as the king (as James Frazer and many of the early anthropologists claimed) was the original "sacred receptacle or victim" who cumulated all of a community's transgressions and guilt into his person. In the original forms of the sacred kingship the king was sacrificed after he accumulated the community's transgressions, just as Freud argued with respect to the father. The original murder, then, was not the father per se but the sacred king. The idea, apparently, was that the sacrifice eliminated the sin along with the victim who contained the full weight of the sins of the community. After kingly sacrifice was eliminated, impurities were thought to cumulate in a sacrificial victim like a prisoner of war or some other scapegoat. Then human sacrifice itself was eliminated and animals became the sacrificial victims. Later still, with the onset of the axial age, impurities were seen as a matter of the interior person, the heart and soul of a person. The person himself then needed to be purified interiorly, spiritually. Impurities could be manifested as demonic possession.

In our day-to-day lives we accumulate sins, transgressions, and impurities. The cumulative effect of these impurities is registered as guilt and this guilt needs to be periodically acknowledged and eliminated via public sacrificial rites if cooperation within the group is going to be possible. When public sacrificial rites are not seen as effective, the full weight of sin of the individual and to some extent of the community has to be carried by the individual him- or herself. In these sorts of historical situations (when sacrificial rites are not seen as effective by the community), individual human beings become more vulnerable to demonic possession as the internal experience of guilt becomes too much to bear.

How does guilt prepare an individual for spirit possession? Of course not everyone who experiences guilt becomes a candidate for spirit possession but only persons with some sense of guilt can become possessed. Why is that? As discussed above, guilt—religious guilt—presupposes an awareness of a discrepancy between current self and ideal self. Spirit possession requires that the individual's sense of current self be radically unstable and only guilt can undermine the ontological stability of the self. Guilt places a question mark over the self. The self must change to end the guilt. Change can be miniscule or profound in proportion to the guilt experienced. The greater the self-awareness of the individual, the greater the capacity for guilt and the greater the potential for profound conversion of self into not-self, hopefully the ideal self.

With respect to possession states, the transformation of the self that guilt calls for leads the individual into perilous waters. That transformation can be either positive or negative; if negative chances are increased then the possession will be demonic. Freud's study of a case of demon possession speaks to the issue of what causes a negative possession experience once guilt triggers a possession event.

FREUD'S CASE STUDY OF DEMON POSSESSION

The case of "demonological neurosis" is the clinical history of Johann Christoph Haitzmann, a painter. The case was offered to Freud by Hofrat Dr. R Payer-Thurn, director of the Imperial Foderkommissbibliothsk of Vienna. Freud was allowed to personally inspect various documents that dealt with Haitzmann's case: a letter of introduction and a manuscript in two parts, one by a monastic compiler, written in Latin, and a fragment from the patient's diary. The diary concerned mostly the period of time (roughly a year) between the first exorcism experience and a "relapse" into demonic possession. Thus the diary recounts the slow reemergence of the possession "neurosis." There were eight illustrations associated with these two texts (the manuscript in Latin and the diary in German) by Haitzmann himself representing times when the devil appeared to Haitzmann.

Haitzmann repeatedly became depressed and was seized with convulsions while attending Mass. The convulsions presumably involved some demonic manifestations as Haitzmann was referred to a "Praefectus Dominii Pottenbrunnensis." The Prefect was apparently responsible in some way for public order. Haitzmann confessed that nine years previously he had been tempted nine times by the devil and then finally gave in by promising in writing to belong to the devil body and soul at the end of nine years. The nine-year deadline was approaching when he had the convulsions in Mass that brought him to the attention of the authorities.

Haitzmann, we are told, regretted his bargain and became convinced that only the intervention of Mary the Virgin Mother of God at the retreat monastery of Mariazell could save his soul and force the devil to release him of his bond. He thus went to Mariazell and in a dramatic set of events produced a paper that was the original "contract" written in blood. Satan had disgorged it but only Haitzmann witnessed the event. Haitzmann, presumably cured, left Mariazell and went to live with his married sister for a year. In that year he kept a diary. A year after the "return" of the pact, however, Haitzmann once again became possessed. He then returned to Mariazell, confessing to the monks that there had been two pacts; one, written in blood, had been retrieved from the devil the year before but another one, in ink, had been written a year or so before the pact written in blood. He then went through a second exorcism, which was successful, and spent the rest of his life in that monastery. Inspection of the history of the case produced by the monastic compiler reveals that Haitzmann was depressed over the recent (i.e., nine years previously) death of his father.

How does Freud theorize this case of demonic possession? In general he asserts that cases of demonic possession in past ages correspond to cases of neuroses of the present day. Evil impulses are no longer projected outwardly to some independent agent but are seen as impulses within the individual. Freud asks, "Why does one sell oneself to the devil?" He rightly remarks that Haitzmann does not require riches, women, or fame from the devil. While it is not clear from the textual sources just what Haitzmann asked of the devil, Freud notes that his major complaints were depression after the death of his father and lack of success at painting. Freud concludes that Haitzmann sold himself to the devil in order to be freed from a state of depression. We can surmise as well that he construed his seizure disorder as related to his melancholia. Thus, he wanted to get well. Anyone who has witnessed an individual who becomes severely depressed will understand this poor man's plight. Riches, fame, and power seem as nothing to someone who cannot feel any pleasure or joy at all.

Freud argues that Haitzmann's depression was due to the death of his father and he cites the wording of the pact with the devil to support this argument "I Christoph Haitzmann sign a deed and pledge myself to be unto this lord even as a son of his body for 9 years." Freud argues that the devil will act as a father substitute for Haitzmann for nine years and then own his soul thereafter. In the illustrations that Haitzmann paints to record the appearances of the devil, he appears first as a typical "honest old burgher"—much as Haitzmann's father himself probably looked before he died. Later the devil appears in more terrifying guises and finally as a dragon. But even if we grant to Freud that the demise of the father contributed to the possession experience, we must ask: why would anyone turn to the devil to act as a father substitute? Freud points out that God himself is referred to as father, so supernatural agents are clothed in the language and imagery of fatherhood. Freud also notes that the child's relations to the father are marked by ambiguity and conflicting impulses: on the one hand love and fondness and on the other hand jealousy (over attentions from the mother and so on), as well as dread and defiance. The devil inherits all the hate, fear, defiance, and dread that the father universally elicits from his children—but none of the love, reverence, and warmth the father also typically elicits from his children. So the devil comes well prepared as a figure upon which to project feelings about the father. Freud speculates that Haitzmann may have had a very conflicted relationship with his father.

> It is possible that the father had opposed his son's wish to become a painter; his incapacity to paint after his father's death would then, on the one hand, be an expression of the familiar "deferred obedience" and on the other by rendering him incapable of making a livelihood it would be bound to increase his longing for the father to stand between him and the cares of life. (Freud 1923, 452)

In his most bold speculation about this case, Freud notes that the number nine recurs repeatedly in the case history. Why? The bond with the devil was for nine years. Haitzmann withstood the temptations of the devil nine times before succumbing and signing the pact. Freud argues that this points to an unconscious fantasy of pregnancy!

> In his mourning for the departed father and its intensification of the longing for him the long since repressed fantasy of pregnancy is reawakened in our painter which he must then defend himself against by means of a neurosis and by denigrating the father. (Freud 1923, 455)

Freud realizes how fanciful most readers will take this explanation for the recurrence of the nine motif:

> Amongst all the observations concerning the mental life of children which psychoanalysis has made, there is hardly one which sounds so repugnant and incredible to the normal adult as the boy's feminine attitude to the father and the fantasy of pregnancy derived from it. (Freud 1923, 456)

So Freud seems to be arguing the following as to why Haitzmann experienced a negative, demonic possession: The patient was depressed over the loss of his father and the loss triggered unresolved emotional conflicts vis-à-vis the father, most particularly the old oedipal urges of murderous rage toward the father on the one hand and deep longing on the other hand for guidance from the father as to how to avoid undue influence from the mother and then to inhibit impulses and become a man. The need for guidance from the father was so great as to trigger a feminine attitude toward the father and unconscious fantasy of pregnancy. When the father died, guilt over harboring conflicting impulses toward the father erupted, which was then masked by the depression. The guilt then destabilized the patient's sense of self and the depression made the ensuing possession negative. In the end Freud concludes,

> Perhaps Christoph Haitzmann was only a poor devil, one of those who never have any luck; perhaps he was too poorly gifted, too ineffective to make a living and belonged to that well known type, the "eternal suckling'—to those who are unable to tear themselves away from the joyous haven at the mother's breast, who hold fast all through their lives to their claim to be nourished by someone else. And so in his illness our painter followed the path from his own father by way of the devil as a father substitute to the pious fathers. (Freud 1923, 470–471)

Perhaps. But then Freud's conclusions concerning Haitzmann leave out too many important facts. First of all there is the seizure disorder. It is a remarkable fact that there is no report of further seizures after the second exorcism. As Freud himself notes, the monastic compilers were willing to report the facts of the case even if it made them look bad. If there were further seizures, why do we not hear about them? If there were no further seizures, then we must conclude that exorcism was effective and that Haitzmann had done more than just settled for monastic life as some sort of refuge from a cruel world! He found something there that freed him of the twin evils of depression and seizures. Surely that is something to admire? Freud's explanation for the origins of the possession seems strained, to say the least. As I mentioned above Freud is right to point to guilt but I think it odd to point to an oedipal complex to explain the guilt. Freud is right to insist on the central role of the father but wrong to insist that guilt emerges in reaction to murderous impulses directed toward the father. Instead, the father's role appears to be to help the child say no to impulses and then to guide the child into that greatest of all gifts: self-awareness. We do not need to posit murderous impulses toward the father in order to arrive at guilt as a constitutive religious emotion. Guilt arises from self-awareness— particularly awareness of a discrepancy between a current and an ideal self. To the extent that the father embodies an ideal future self for the child the father will be connected with the guilt but the essential factor is the awareness of falling short of an ideal. No future can exist unless the individual can escape from or inhibit current impulses and here the father is crucial. He shows the child just how do delay gratification.

So why did Haitzmann become demonically possessed? Beyond saying that he must have been a courageous man and a very self-aware man with some awareness of guilt, we can say very little. The stresses of work, depression, familial loss, and a seizure disorder did not help. As we will see in many other cases of demonic possession these sorts of stresses can tip the balance toward negative possession, but the core psychologic key to negative possession is an acute awareness of guilt. We know from the manuscript sources that Haitzmann was acutely troubled by his lack of success in painting. Freud speculates that his father may have opposed his son's wish to be a painter. Alternatively, the father may have urged the son to become a great painter and when the son fell short of that ideal he felt guilty. He knew he had the capacity but he failed to realize that capacity and that caused him guilt. To have talent and not to fully realize it is one of the most painful experiences imaginable. It is also one way that human beings come to guilt and guilt in turn triggers religious consciousness and whole new possibilities.

Chapter 4

 Cases with Commentary

I would like now to review a variety of case studies of demonic possession. These case descriptions will give the reader a vivid picture of what a case of demon possession really looks like. Some are taken from Oesterreich's book (1922/1974) as this is the largest compendium of cases ever collated by a scientist (rather than a theologian) into a single volume that is easily available in English. But I also include cases from other sources, including the scientific literature.

The purpose of this review is to illustrate some of the characteristics of demonic possession that I have discussed in past chapters (presence of guilt as a motivating factor, female predominance, display of primitive impulses, super-normal powers, etc.) and to demonstrate that demonic possession is a phenomenon that has its own laws of unity, its own specific cognitive, behavioral, and emotional content and phenomenology. It is not reducible to any other category like somnambulism, dissociative identity disorder, epilepsy, mania, depression, Tourette's syndrome, and so on. All of these disorders can certainly be part of the picture of demonic possession but the possession phenomena go beyond the normal presentation of any one of these disorders and constitute a behavioral display that is sui generis. The specific unity of demonic possession is as described in previous chapters of this book. It involves the temporary displacement of the primary identity and a transfer of control to a demonic identity. There is an aversion to sacred things (however the culture defines them) and a display of socially inappropriate behaviors that can take many forms. There is a marked guilt-induced form of self-destructiveness. There is an increased frequency of nightmares. There is a paradoxical decrease in social interests and competence and an increase in unusual cognitive abilities. The latter can sometime seem uncanny or paranormal (as when one of the demoniacs told King James of a secret conversation he had had with his future queen). There are tremendous and paradoxical physical changes where the individual's health rapidly declines while the individual may nevertheless possess extraordinary physical strength. There are marked changes in posture, ambulation, and dramatic changes in the voice of the possessed—for example, female voices became male voices or one voice becomes two or more.

As discussed previously, provisional potential physiologic explanation for all of these changes associated with demonic possession is that there is either a preexisting reduction in brain asymmetry or a new onset disorder of some kind that leads to a reduction in asymmetry. This reduction in asymmetry makes it more difficult for the individual to sequester or insulate cognitive processes from one another. Cognitive blends become more frequent, leading to an increase in unusual cognitive outputs that might involve everything from manic chains of associative trains of thought where everything seems to be related to everything else to production of new metaphors and religious imagery to outright bizarre delusions and nightmares. The reduction in asymmetry and the resultant blending of cognitive processes also involves the disinhibition of REM sleep physiology and the irruption of dreams and nightmares into waking consciousness. The reduction in asymmetry also leads to a marked reduction in the sense of agency and this reduction facilitates the sense of loss of self and invasion and control by a new entity. Thus the brain dysfunction yields the major events that make a person vulnerable to identity disorder and delusional ideations. But why does the individual cast the whole experience in religious terms? Why is the possessing entity demonic? Here is where culture enters into the picture. If the individual is living in a culture where the sacrificial rites have broken down and lost their ability to inspire awe and reverence, then individual persons offer themselves up as sacrificial offerings. To do so they must take on the sins and transgressions and impurities of all those around them and then they must find a way to kill or destroy the sin by destroying themselves. Sometimes the destruction will be of both host and demon—sometimes only the demon will be destroyed via the exorcism. In traditional cultures exorcism or destruction of the demon was always via use of a fetish object that could trap and imprison the demon forever. In Christian societies the exorcism itself is understood to banish the demon back to hell or somewhere where it could not harm the individual anymore. In short, a portion of the symptoms or phenomenology of demonic possession (such as the reduction in agency, the cognitive and motor changes) comes from the brain disorder and the other portion of the experience comes from the cultural matrix around sacrificial rites. It is important to point out that when I use the term *brain disorder* I simply mean that. Disorder is being used here descriptively as a state variable not as a clinical entity. The "disorder" is reversible.

What kind of person willingly (subconsciously, of course) takes on the impurities of others so as to eliminate them from the community? A self-sacrificial person. A person who has been socialized to carry the weaknesses and defects of others. A person willing to give him- or herself for others. These are often religious people or people who score high on altruism, compassion, and empathy scales. Women are socialized to be both self-giving and self-sacrificial, they have less symmetrical brains than their male counterparts, and they tend to be more religious than men. It should not be surprising, therefore, that women are more often demonically possessed than men. On the other hand, many soldiers and policemen and firemen willingly put their lives on the line for others every day so these individuals would also be candidates to (subconsciously) voluntarily take on the impurities and transgressions of others in order to purge them from the community. In any case, how can we sum up the unity and the essence of the phenomenon of demonic possession? I would put it this way: *Demonic possession involves a dramatic transfer of agency from the everyday Self to an impure but cognitively extraordinary Self that needs to be publicly displayed and then destroyed.* I will show that the following case studies will support this characterization. Note that there are four basic elements to this characterization of the demonic possession state: (1) transferral of agency (2) to an impure/but cognitively extraordinary Self (3) that needs to be publicly displayed and (4) then destroyed.

The transferral of agency to a demonic identity, of course, is the prerequisite of the possession experience itself. The old identity is buried in order to make room for the sacrificial victim. The idea is to create a receptacle (identity) that can contain all the impurities of the community. Only a supernatural being can contain the sins of the entire community so the new identity is a demon. The new identity is filled with filth and sin but is also cognitively extraordinary in that he can read minds, predict futures, translocate, and so on. These elements are necessary because once again the sacrificial victim has to be divine in some sense in order to make the sacrifice useful for the whole community; only a supernatural being can contain the sins of the entire community. The demon has to be destroyed or exorcised to make the whole drama worthwhile. Sacrifice or the destruction and elimination of impurities is the aim of the whole enterprise. Exorcism is the destruction of the demon. Paradoxically, then, demonic possession is an attempt at purification—not just of self but of a whole community.

We will see all four of the elements above in every genuine case of demonic possession. Destruction of the demon is the goal. Exorcism is the usual method. Sometimes it works, sometimes it doesn't. It works in the same proportion that the individual believes in the power of the ritual. That is a difficult feat in a culture where sacrificial rites more generally are seen as ineffective. The demonically possessed are therefore doubly unfortunate. The lack of reverence in the general culture for the ancient sacrificial rites makes them vulnerable to becoming victims themselves. Their self-sacrificial character, so noble a trait in itself, makes them vulnerable to possession. Once they are possessed, however, their well-being then becomes dependent on the strength of the exorcism rituals, but these religious rituals too are subject, just like the sacrificial rites, to that cultural erosion of belief in and reverence for the ritual itself. Usually, however, the people most vulnerable to possession are the people who are self-sacrificial and intensely religious to begin with. These are the individuals who still strongly believe in the ancient rituals even when no one else holds them in awe. These are the individuals who are the strong ones, the ones strong enough to offer themselves as sacrificial victims. They can take on the sins of the community, suffer them for a while, help destroy them, and still come out alive! Let us now look at some cases.

Case 1

The patient was a peasant-woman of thirty-four years. . . . Her past life up to this time had been irreproachable. She kept her house and showed due regard for religion without being especially devout. Without any definite cause which could be discovered, she was seized in August, 1830, by terrible fits of convulsions, during which a strange voice began to speak (it professed to be that of an unhappy dead man), her individuality vanished, to give place to another. So long as this lasted she knew nothing of her individuality, which only reappeared (in all its integrity and reason) when she had retired to rest. This demon shouted, swore, and raged in the most terrible fashion. He broke out especially into curses against God and everything sacred. Bodily measures and medicines did not produce the slightest change in her state, nor did a pregnancy and the suckling which followed it. Only continual prayer (to which moreover she was obliged to apply herself with the greatest perseverance, for the demon could not endure it) often frustrated the demon for a time. During five months all the resources of medicine were tried in vain. . . . On the contrary, two demons now spoke in her; who often, as it were, played the raging multitude within her, barked like dogs, mewed like cats, etc. Did she begin to pray, the demons at once flung her into the air, swore, and made a horrible din through her mouth.

When the demons left her in peace she came to herself, and on hearing the accounts of those present, and seeing the injuries inflicted upon her by blows and falls, she burst into sobs and lamented her condition. By a magico-magnetic (that is to say, hypnotic) treatment . . . one of the demons had been expelled before she was brought to me; but the one who remained only made the more turmoil. Prayer was also particularly disagreeable to this one. If the woman wished to kneel down to pray, the demon strove to prevent her with all his might, and if she persisted he forced her jaws apart and obliged her to utter a diabolic laugh or whistle. . . .

She was able to eat nothing but a soup of black bread and water. As soon as she took anything better, the demon rose up in her and cried: "Carrion should eat nothing good!" and took away her plate. She often fasted for two or three complete days without taking a crumb of food and without drinking a drop. One those days the demon kept quiet. Through distress, suffering and fasting, she had grown thin and was little more than a skeleton. Her pains were often so great, by night as well as by day, as to beggar description, and we like herself were in despair over them. (Oesterreich 1974, 14–15)

Comment: The transferral of agency is clear in this case and it is dramatic. In the evenings she was herself . . . a somewhat religious woman but not overly so. The demonic identity actually involved two identities. One of the demons had been eliminated via hypnosis but the other identity was not so easily disposed of. My own feeling is that an exorcism will not work until the demon has been allowed to display its impurity, its maliciousness. After all, the purpose of demonic possession is sacrificial. The victim takes on the sins of the people around him or her in order to eliminate those sins. The sacrifice, however, will not be effective; it will not have a salutary effect on the community unless the community or its representatives witness the sacred victim and its destruction. In this case we also get clear evidence that the victim is self-destructive. This is to be expected if she is being prepared for the sacrifice. The sacrifice is the exorcism ritual, but if that is not effective then the victim becomes physically self-destructive.

Case 2

In this state the eyes were tightly shut, the face grimacing, often excessively and horribly changed, the voice repugnant, full of shrill cries, deep groans, coarse words; the speech expressing the joy of inflicting hurt or cursing God and the universe, addressing terrible threats now to the doctor, now to the patient herself, saying with deliberate and savage obstinacy that he would not abandon the body of this poor woman and that he would torture both her and her near ones more and more. Thus she was one day constrained by the demon to beat her beloved child, when during one of the attacks he knelt down beside his mother to pray for her. The most dreadful thing was the way in which she raged when she had to submit to be touched or rubbed down during the fits; she defended herself with her hands, threatening all those who approached, insulting and abusing them in the vilest terms; her body bent backwards like a bow was flung out of the chair and writhed upon the ground, then lay there stretched out at full length, stiff and cold, assuming the very appearance of death. If in spite of her resistance anyone succeeded in administering something to the patient she at once manifested a violent movement to vomit up again what had been forced upon her. This occurred each time with diabolic howlings and a terrible panting, alternating with satanic bursts of laughter in a piercing falsetto. (Oesterreich 1974, 22)

Comment: The transferral of agency is clear when contrasting the mother of a "beloved son" versus the savage demon beating the child for prayer for his mother! The accent in this case is on display, violent display of violent hatreds, particularly against sacred things. The display of the demonic self is dramatic and thus attempts to destroy that self are correspondingly dramatic. The exorcism is ineffectual so she tries to harm herself and those around her. It should be obvious that in all cases of possession there is likely a background of brain disorder that often involves the motor system. That is the source of tics, violent, involuntary movements, and so forth. But, as argued above, the brain disorder is not the whole story.

Case 3

The patient was a Spanish abbess who was involved in an epidemic of possession at Madrid (1628–1631).

When I began to find myself in this state I felt within me movements so extraordinary that I judged the cause could not be natural. I recited several orisons asking God to deliver me from such terrible pain. Seeing that my state did not change, I several times begged the prior to exorcise me; as he was not willing to do so and sought to turn me from it, telling me that all I related was only the outcome of my imagination, I did all that lay in me to believe it, but the pain drove me to feel the contrary. At length on the day of Our Lady the prior took a stole, and after having offered up several prayers, asked God to reveal to me whether the demon was in my body by unmasking him, or else to take away these sufferings and this pain which I felt anything, I suddenly fell into a sort of swooning and delirium, doing and saying things of which the idea had never occurred to me in my life. I began to feel this state when I had placed on my head the wood, which seemed as heavy as a tower. This continued in the same way during three months and I rarely felt myself in my normal and natural state. Nature had given me so tranquil a character that even in childhood I was quite unlike my age and loved neither the games, liveliness, nor movement habitual to it. Accordingly it could not but be regarded as a supernatural thing that having reached the age of twenty-six years and become a nun and even an abbess, I committed follies of which I had never before been capable. . . .

It sometimes happened that the demon Peregrino [that is, the sister possessed by this devil, who played part of superior to the devils] was in the second-floor dormitory when I was in the parlour, and he would say: "Is Dona Teresa with the visitors? I will soon make her come. . . ." I did not hear these words, but felt inwardly an inexpressible uneasiness, and rapidly took previous deliberation. I then felt the presence of the demon who was in my body; I began without thinking to run, muttering, "Lord Peregrino calls me"; so I came where the demon was, and before arriving there was already speaking of whatever thing they had under discussion and of which I had had no previous knowledge. . . .

Some people said that we feigned to be in that state through vanity, and I specially to gain the affection of my nuns and other serious persons; but in order to be convinced that it was not this sentiment which actuated us it suffices to know that out of our full number of thirty nuns there were twenty-five who were in this state, and that of the five others three were my best friends. As for outside persons, we were in a state more likely to inspire them with fear than to make us beloved and sought after. (Oesterreich 1974, 41)

Comment: This abbess speaks with frankness and we must take her at her word. She is, after all, claiming only a single extraordinary capacity, that of precognition, of knowing what people in another location are talking about. Whether or not we believe that this capacity is real or was real in the case of this abbess, she believes it to be true. The demon is a supernatural being and he must sometimes display extraordinary cognitive capacities to prove that he is supernatural. It is interesting that the possession of this abbess was part of a mass hysterical set of possession among most of the nuns in this convent. Mass possession among nuns and other female religious should not be surprising as these women, if they have any piece of a real vocation to the religious life, are self-sacrificial. They obviously also believe in the supernatural and in the efficacy of ritual exorcism to eliminate impurity and sin from a community. Religious women, therefore, are most at risk for demonic possession.

Case 4

A young gentleman used from time to time to fall into a certain convulsion, having now the left arm alone, now a single finger, now one thigh, now both, now the backbone and the whole body so suddenly shaken and tormented by this convulsion that only with great difficulty could four menservants hold him down in bed. Now it is a fact that his intellect was in no way disturbed nor tormented: his speech was untrammeled, his mind not at all confused, and he was in full possession of all his senses, even at the height of this convulsion. He was racked at least twice a day by the said convulsion, on coming out of which he was quite well except that he felt prostrate with fatigue by reason of the torments which he had suffered. Any skilled doctor might have judged that is was a true epilepsy if the senses or the mind had been deranged withal. All the best doctors being called in, judged that it was a convulsion approaching very nearly to epilepsy which was excited by a malignant vapour enclosed in the backbone, from whence the said vapour spread only to those nerves which have their origin in the backbone, without in any way attacking the brain. This judgment having been formed as to the cause of the sickness, nothing of what the art prescribes was left undone to relieve this poor sick man; but in vain we put forth all our efforts, being more than a hundred leagues from the cause of the malady.

For in the third month they discovered that is was a devil who was the author of this ill, who declared himself of his own accord, speaking freely by the mouth of the sick man in Latin and Greek, although this latter had no knowledge of Greek. He discovered the secrets of those who were there present, and principally of the doctors, mocking at them because with useless medicines they had almost caused the death of the sufferer. Any and every time that his father came to see him, as soon as he saw him from afar he cried out: "Make him go away, do not let him come in, or else take from him the chain round his neck," for being a knight he wore, accordingly to the custom of the French knights, the collar of the Order from which hung the image of St. Michael. When aught from the Holy Scriptures was read in his presence he became much more irritated, indignant, and agitated than before. When the paroxysm had passed the poor tormented man remembered all that he had done and said, repenting thereof and saying that against his will he had done or said those things. (Oesterreich 1974, 48)

Comment: This case is interesting because of the acute observation of those attending the patient. The condition could not have been traditional epilepsy. The man obviously had some sort of motor disorder and seizures but it is still not clear what disease he had. The case is also interesting in that the demonic self had once again to display extraordinary cognitive capacities.

We turn next to a discussion of the possessions at a convent in Loudun, France in 1630–1634. The nuns at this convent claimed demonic possession due to the bewitchment of a priest named Grandier. Grandier was tried for sorcery and brutally tortured and executed because of the nuns' hysterical accusations. The abbess in this case was Sister Jeanne des Anges. She was the chief attraction because her displays of demonic possession were the most elaborate. Even though she recanted her accusations against Grandier, he was nevertheless executed. She later repented her actions to some extent and appears to have taken to the religious life more seriously than she did when she first entered the convent. She wrote an autobiographical account of her possession experiences. We will examine the passages Oesterreich saw fit to quote. We will also look at the subsequent possession experiences of one of Sister Jeanne's exorcists, Father Surin. Though Oesterreich does not comment on this facet of the cases, the two possessions are extremely fascinating as they were by the same demon or demons. Father Surin had failed to exorcise the demons from Sister Jeanne until he offered to take them on himself. That is, he offered himself up as a sacrificial victim in place of the abbess. The demons entered Surin and left Jeanne. She, in fact, thereafter ceased her demonic performances and actually became a more exemplary religious person—though she always evidenced a strain of vanity and self-delusion. Despite her character flaws her account of her possessions is interesting especially when juxtaposed with Surin's, as we will see, beginning with Sister Jeanne's account.

Case 5

At the commencement of my possession I was almost three months in a continual disturbance of mind, so that I do not remember anything of what passed during that time. The demons acted with abounding force and the Church fought them day and night with exorcisms.

My mind was often filled with blasphemies and sometimes I uttered them without being able to take any thought to stop myself. I felt for God a continual aversion and nothing inspired me with greater hatred than the spectacle of his goodness and the readiness with which he pardons repentant sinners. My thoughts were often bent on devising ways to displease him and to make other trespass against him. It is true that by the mercy of God I was not free in these sentiments, although at that time I did not know it, for the demon beclouded me in such a way that I hardly distinguished his desires from mine; he gave me, moreover, a strong aversion for my religious calling, so that sometimes when he was in my head I tore all my veils and such of my sisters' as I could lay hands on; I trampled them underfoot, I chewed them, cursing the hour when I took the vows. All this was done with great violence, I think that I was not free.

. . . As I went up for Communion the devil took possession of my hand, and when I had received the Sacred Host and had half moistened it the devil flung it into the priest's face. I know full well that I did not do this action freely, but I am fully assured to my deep confusion that I gave the devil occasion to do it. I think he would not have had this power if I had not been in league with him. I have on several other occasions had similar experiences for when I resisted them stoutly I found that all these furies and rages dispersed as they had come, but alas, it too often happened that I did not strongly constrain myself to resist, especially in matters where I saw no grievous sin. But this is where I deluded myself, for because I did not restrain myself in little things my mind was afterwards taken unawares in great ones. . . .

At this reply the evil spirit got into such a fury that I thought he would kill me; he beat me with great violence so that my face was quite disfigured and my body all bruised with his blows. It often happened that he treated me in this way. As for outward things, I was much troubled by almost continual rages and fits of madness. I found myself almost incapable of doing any good thing, seeing that I had not an hour of the liberty to think of my conscience and prepare myself for a general confession although God caused me to be moved towards it and I was so minded. (Oesterreich 1974, 49–50)

Comment: In this famous case of possession, if we can take Sister Jeanne at her word, there was a marked aversion to things of God or purity and an attraction to things impure. There was extreme self-destructiveness and extreme public displays of demonic activity. Though not recounted here the exorcisms of the abbess and her nuns were performed in front of a public audience. Sometimes that audience included high royalty like the brother of the king of France.

In the following testimony from Father Surin we get a very vivid description of the loss of agency and self during demonic possession. Father Surin had voluntarily taken on the demons that had possessed Sister Jeanne but the demons in this case affected the man's interior life more than his outward behaviors. There was, of course, a profound reduction in agency and behavioral output but there were no displays for the public outside of his religious community. Exorcisms were unavailing in his case. He endured years of what appears to be a profound depression or apathy. The demon was destroyed ultimately by "prayer and fasting"—a formula recommended by Jesus himself for certain types of cases.

Case 6

Father Surin's chief testimony is a letter to a spiritual friend written on May 3, 1635:

There are scarce any persons to whom I take pleasure in recounting my adventures, save your Reverence, who listens to them willingly and derives from them reflections which would not readily occur to others who do not know me as does your Reverence. Since the last letter which I wrote you I have fallen into a state very different from anything I had anticipated, but in full conformity with the Providence of God concerning my soul. I am no longer at Merennes, but at Loudun, where I received your letter recently. I am in perpetual conversation with the devils, in the course of which I have been subject to happenings which would be too lengthy to relate to you and which have given me more reason than I ever had to know and to admire the goodness of God. I wish to tell you something of them, and would tell you more if you were more private. I have engaged in combat with four of the most potent and malicious devils in hell. I, I say, whose infirmities you know. God had permitted the struggles to be so fierce and the onslaughts so frequent that exorcism was the least of the battlefields, for the enemies declared themselves in private both by night and day in a thousand different ways. You may imagine what pleasure there is in finding oneself at the sole mercy of God. I will tell you no more, it suffices that knowing my state you should take occasion to pray for me. At all events, for the last three and a half months I have never been without a devil at work upon me.

Things have gone so far that God has permitted, I think for my sins, what has perhaps never been seen in the Church, that in the exercise of my ministry the devil passes out of the body of the possessed woman and entering into mine assaults and confounds me, agitates and troubles me visibly, possessing me for several hours like a demoniac. I cannot explain to you what happens within me during that time and how this spirit unites with mine without depriving me either of consciousness or liberty or soul, nevertheless making himself like another me and as if I had two souls, one of which is dispossessed of its body and the use of its organs and stands aside watching the actions of the other which has entered into them. The two spirits fight in one and the same field which is the body, and the soul is as if divided. According to one of its parts it is subject to diabolic impression and according to the other to those motions which are proper to it or granted by God. At the same time I feel a great peace under God's good pleasure and, without knowing how it arises, and extreme rage and aversion for him, giving rise to violent impulses to cut myself off from him which astonish the beholder; at the same time a great joy and sweetness, and on the other hand a wretchedness which manifests itself by cries and lamentations like those of the demons; I feel the state of damnation and apprehend it, and feel myself as if transpierced by the arrows of despair in that stranger soul which seems to be mine, while the other soul which is full of confidence laughs at such feeling and is at full liberty to curse him who is the cause; I even feel that the same cries which issue from my mouth come equally from the two souls, and am at a loss to discern whether they be caused by joy or by the extreme fury with which I am filled. The trembling with which I am seized when the Holy Sacrament is administered to me arise equally, so far as I can judge, from horror of its presence which is insufferable to me and from a sincere and meek reverence, without it being possible for me to attribute them to the one rather than the other or to check them. When I desire by the motion of one of these two souls to make the sign of the cross on my mouth, the other averts my hand with great swiftness and grips my finger in its teeth to bite me with rage. I scarcely ever find orisons easier or more tranquil than I these agitations; while the body rolls upon the ground and the ministers of the Church speak to me as to a devil, loading me with malediction, I cannot tell you the joy that I feel, having become a devil not by rebellion against God but by the calamity which shows me plainly the state to which sin has reduced me and how that taking to myself all the curses which are heaped upon me my soul has reason to sink in its own nothingness. When the other possessed persons see me in this state it is a pleasure to see how they triumph and how the devils mock at me saying: "Physician, heal thyself; go now and climb into the pulpit; it will be a fine sight to see him preach after he had rolled upon the ground." *Tentaverun, subsannaverunt me subsannatione, freduerunt super me dentibus suis.*

What a cause for thankfulness that I should thus see myself the sport of the (evil) spirits, and that the justice of God on earth should take vengeance on my sins! What a privilege to experience the state from which Jesus Christ has delivered me, and to feel how great is the redemption, no longer by hearsay but by the impress of that same state; and how good it is to have at once the capacity to fathom that misery and to thank the goodness which has delivered us from it with so many labours! This is what I am now reduced to almost every day. It is the subject of great disputes, and *factus sum magna quoestio*, whether there is possession or not, and if it may be that such untoward accidents befall the ministers of Gospel. Some say that it is a chastisement of God upon me to punish an error; others say some other thing, and I am content and would not change my fortune with another, having the firm persuasion that there is nothing better than to be reduced to great extremities. That in which I am is such that I can do few things freely: when I wish to speak my speech is cut off; at Mass I am brought up short; at table I cannot carry the morsel to my mouth; at confession I suddenly forget my sins; and I feel the devil come and go within me as if he were at home. As soon as I wake he is there; at orisons he distracts my thoughts when he pleases; when my heart begins to swell with the presence of God he fills it with rage; he makes me sleep when I would wake; and, publicly, by the mouth of the possessed woman he boast of being my master; the which I can in no way contradict. Enduring the reproach of my conscience and upon my head the sentence pronounced against sinners, I must suffer it and revere the order of Divine Providence to which every creature must bow. It is not a single demon who torments me; there are usually two, the one is Leviathan, the adversary of the Holy Spirit, for according to what they have said here, they have in hell a trinity whom the magicians worship: Lucifer, Beelzebub, and Leviathan, who is third in hell, as some authors have already observed and written. Now the works of this false Paraclete are quite contrary to those of the true, and impart a desolation which cannot be adequately described. He is the chief of all our band of demons and has command of this whole affair which is perhaps one of the strangest ever seen. In this same place we see Paradise and Hell, nuns who taken in one way are like Ursula and in the other worse than the most abandoned in all sorts of disorders, filth, blasphemy, and rages. If it please you Reverence, I do not at all desire that you should make my letter public. You are the only one to whom, except for my confessor and my superiors, I have been willing to say so much. It is but to maintain between us such communication as may assist us to glorify God in whom I am your very humble servant.

Jean-Joseph Surin

And by way of post-scriptum, I beg you to have prayers said for me of which I have need, for during whole weeks I am so stupid toward heavenly things that I should be glad if someone would make me say my prayers like a child and explain the *Pater Noster* to me simply. The devil has said to me: "I will deprive thee of everything and thou shalt have need to keep thy faith for I will make thee besotted." He has made a pact with a witch to prevent me from speaking of God and so that he may have strength to keep my spirit broken, and I am constrained, in order to have some understanding, to hold the Holy Sacrament often against my head, using David's key to unlock my memory. . . .

I am confident to die since Our Lord has done me this grace to have retrieved three consecrated Hosts which three witches had delivered into the hands of the devil, who brought them back to me publicly from Paris where they were under the mattress of a bed and left the Church in possession of this honour, to have given back in some measure to her Redeemer what she had received of Him, having ransomed it from the devil's clutches. I do not know if Our Lord will soon take my life, for being hard put to it in this affair I gave it to Him and promised to part with it for the price of these three Hosts. It seemed that the devil, but the bodily ills which he inflicts on me, desires to exercise his right and gradually wear me out. (Oesterreich 1974, 51–53)

Comment: Surin's case fits perfectly with our definition of demonic possession: "Demonic possession involves a dramatic transfer of agency from the everyday Self to an impure but cognitively extraordinary Self that needs to be publicly displayed and then destroyed." In Surin we have an intelligent man with a genius for self-observation. He provides a vivid description of what it feels like to lose one's sense of personal agency, and being acutely aware of the loss of agency. Lesions to the supplementary motor area sometimes produce cases of this sort of loss of agency without loss of consciousness. In cases of "alien hand syndrome" one hand may be buttoning up a shirt while the other attempts to unbutton the shirt. One hand may seek to open a door while the other wants to close it and so on. There are extreme cases where one hands attempts to inflict harm on the individual while the other tries to stop that self-mutilation. Something similar seems to have happened to Surin. He underwent demonic possession by voluntarily taking on himself the demons that had possessed Sister Jeanne. He then experienced a profound loss of agency and a transferral of agency over to the demonic entities. His will then battled with the demonic will in very vivid fashion. Surin appears to explicitly conceptualize the demonic possession experience as self-sacrificial. In his writing he evinces a gratefulness to be allowed to suffer for the greater good. Being the sacrificial victim who takes on the sins of others he directly experiences "damnation" but, given his awareness that the possession is a sacrificial experiences, he also simultaneously experiences "how great is the redemption" derived from the sacrifice.

Surin's subsequent history was one of at least 25 years of suffering until he finally experienced release from the power of the demons. His sufferings became so acute at one point that he seriously considered suicide. But eventually his despair gave way to triumph and he died a saintly man.

Case 7

We next turn to a case of the famous French psychiatrist Pierre Janet (1859–1947).

The patient is a man of thirty-three years who was brought to the Saltpêtrière four years ago in Charcot's time. I was able closely to examine this person confided to my care, and was fortunate enough to restore his reason completely in a few months. The cure has been maintained for more than three years and the patient has been followed up for a sufficient length of time to render it possible now to study his delirium, examining the means which effected the cure and which may be called modern exorcism, and finally to extract from this observation the maximum of information possible. There is, moreover, no objection to my relating the misadventures of this unfortunate man; I will give him a false name and change that of his native place together with his social position; the psychological and medical facts alone will be accurate. . . . Achille, as we will call him, belonged to a family of peasants in a small way in the south of France; he was brought up amongst simple people evidently without much education. This confirms Esquirol's remark that the delirium of possession is to-day practically confined to the lower classes. His parents and the villagers were superstitiously inclined and strange legends were current about his family. His father was accused of having at some previous time given himself to the devil and of going every Saturday to an old tree-trunk to converse with Satan who handed him a bag of money. . . . Achille was hereditarily predisposed to insanity . . .; he was a degenerate in the classic sense of the word.

Achille had a normal childhood; he was educated in a little grammar school and showed himself studious and diligent although of only average intelligence; he had in particular a very good memory and read voraciously without much selection. He was sensitive to impressions, took everything seriously "as if it had really happened," as he said, and remained upset for a long time after a fright, a punishment, or the slightest incident. He did not share the superstitions of his village and even had very few religious beliefs. He might have been declared almost normal had he not frequently had sick headaches and had certain small facts which seem to me have their significance not been observed. Although very sensitive and affectionate he did not succeed in making friends, but was always alone and rather an object of ridicule to his schoolfellows. . . . Achille, having left school early . . . engaged in a small business. . . . A very fortunate thing for him was that he married early, towards the age of twenty-two years, a kindly and devoted woman who corrected several imaginative aberrations and made him sensible and happy for several years. He had one child, a little girl who grew up absolutely normal, and everything went well with him for about ten years. Achille was thirty-three years old when he experienced a series of accidents which brought him in the course of a few months to the Saltpêtrière. . . . Towards the end of the winter of 1890 Achille had to make a short journey necessitated by his business, and returned home at the end of a few weeks. Although he said he was quite well and made efforts to appear in good spirits, his wife found him changed. He was gloomy, preoccupied, he scarcely ever kissed his

wife and child and spoke very little. At the end of several days this
taciturnity increased and the poor man had difficulty in muttering
a few words during the course of a day. But his silence assumed a
quite peculiar aspect: it ceased to be voluntary as at first; Achille was
no longer silent because he did not wish to speak, but because he
was not able to speak. He made fruitless efforts to utter a sound and
could no longer manage it; he had become dumb. The doctor con-
sulted shook his head and found the case very grave; he tested the
heart, examined the urine, and concluded that it was general debil-
ity, a modification in the humours, dyscrasia, perhaps diabetes, etc.,
etc. The fear of all these drove Achille to distraction—he rapidly
recovered his speech in order to complain of all sorts of pains. . . .
As at the end of a full month there was no perceptible improvement,
Achille went to consult another doctor (who diagnosed angina pec-
toris). The unfortunate man took to his bed and was overcome by
the blackest depression. He no longer did anything and moreover
no longer understood a word of what he read, often seeming unable
even to grasp the remarks addressed to him. To all the questions of
his despairing wife, he replied that the did not know what depressed
him in this way, that he still kept a stout heart, but that in spite of
himself he felt the most gloomy presentiments. He slept from time
to time, but even in sleep his lips moved and murmured incom-
prehensible words while tears streamed from his eyes. At length
his presentiments appeared to be realized. One day when he was
more depressed than usual he called his wife and child, embraced
them despairingly, then stretched himself upon his bed and made no
further movement. He remained thus motionless during two days
while those who watched beside him expected at every movement
to see him breathe his last. Suddenly, one morning, after two days
of apparent death, Achille arose, sat up with both eyes wide open,
and broke into a frightful laugh. It was a convulsive laugh which
shook his whole body, a laugh of unnatural violence which twisted
his mouth, a lugubrious laugh which lasted for more than two hours
and was truly satanic. From that moment everything was changed.
Achille leapt out of bed and refused all attention. To every question
he replied: "Do nothing, it is useless, let us drink champagne, it is the
end of the world." Then he uttered horrible cries, "They are burning
me, they are cutting me to pieces." These cries and wild movements
lasted until the evening, then the unhappy man fell into a troubled
sleep. The reawakening was no better; Achille related to his assembled family a thousand dreadful things. The demon, said he, was

in the room, surrounded by a crowd of little horned and grimacing imps; still worse, the devil was within him and forced him to
utter horrible blasphemies. In fact Achille's mouth, for he declared
that he had nothing to do with it, abused God and the saints and
repeated a confused mass of the most filthy insults to religion. Yet
graver and more cruel was the fact that the demon twisted his legs
and arms and caused him the most hideous sufferings which wrung
horrible cries from the poor wretch. This was thought to be a state
of high fever with transitory delirium, but the condition was last-
ing. Achille but rarely had calmer moments when he embraced his
daughter, weeping and deploring his sad fate which had made him
the prey of demons. He never expressed the least doubt as to his possession by the devil, of which he was absolutely convinced. "I have
not believed sufficiently in our holy religion nor in the devil," he
often said; "he has taken a terrible revenge, he has me, he is within
me and will never leave me."

When he was not watched, Achille escaped from the house, ran
across the fields, hid in the woods where he was found the next day
completely terrified. He tried especially to get into the cemetery, and
several times was found lying asleep upon a grave. He seemed to
long for death for he took poisons; he swallowed laudanum and part
of a little bottle of Fowler's drops; he even tied his feet together and
thus bound threw himself into a pond. He nevertheless managed to
get out, and when found on the edge said sadly: "You can see well
enough that I am possessed by the devil, since I cannot die. I have
made the test demanded by religion, thrown myself into the water
with my feet tied together, and I floated. Ah, the devil is certainly in
me!" It was necessary to shut him up in his room and watch him
closely; after three months of this raving, which terrified his poor
family, they had to make up their minds, somewhat tardily and on
the advice of a wise doctor, to take him to the Saltpêtrière as the most
propitious place to-day for the exorcism of the possessed and the
expulsion of demons. When Charcot and my friend Mr. Dutil, who
was the head of his clinic, handed over this interesting case to me, I
at once remarked in him all the recognized signs of possession as
described in the medieval epidemics. . . . He [Achille] muttered blasphemies in a muffled and solemn voice: "Cursed be God," said he,
"cursed the Trinity, cursed the Virgin!" . . . then in a shrill voice and
with eyes full of tears: "It is not my fault if my mouth says these horrible things, it is not I. . . . I press my lips together so that the words
may not escape, may not break out, but it's no use, I can feel plainly

that he says them and makes my tongue speak in spite of me. . . . It is the devil who drives me to do all these other things," said Achille again. "I do not want to die, and he drives me against my will to make away with myself. . . . For instance, he is speaking to me at this moment . . ." and he resumes in his deep voice: "Priests are a worthless lot!" then in his high voice: "No, I won't believe it!" and there he was talking with the devil and arguing with him. It often happened that he disputed in this way with his demon who had the bad habit of criticizing him incessantly. "You lie," said the devil to him. "No, I am not lying," replied the poor man. . . . The possessed did not merely feel the action of the devil within themselves, they saw and heard him. Achille did the same. . . . These signs and especially the last (insensibility) also existed in the case of the unfortunate Achille. True, his insensibility was not continuous, but when he twisted his arms in convulsive movements, they could be pricked and pinched without his observing it. . . . When I tried to comfort the poor man and calm him a little I was extremely ill received: all my efforts were useless. I vainly sought to gain an ascendancy over Achille, to force him to obey me; as a last resource I tried whether it was not possible to send him to sleep in order to have more power over him in a hypnotic state; all in vain, I was unable by any means to suggest or hypnotize him; he answered me with insults and blasphemies, and the devil, speaking by his mouth, mocked my impotence. . . . At my special request the almoner of the Saltpêtrière was good enough to see the patient, and also tried to console him and teach him to distinguish true religion from those diabolic superstitions; he had no success and told me that the poor man was mad and rather needed the help of medicine than of religion. I had to try again. I then observed that the patient made many movements unconsciously and that, absorbed in his hallucinations and ravings, he was extremely absentminded. It was easy to take advantage of his absence of mind to produce in his limbs movements which he executed unwittingly. We all know those absent-minded people who look everywhere for the umbrella which they are meanwhile holding without knowing it. I was able to slip a pencil into the fingers of his right hand and Achille gripped and held it without noticing anything. I gently directed the hand which held the pencil and made him write a few strokes, a few letters, and the hand, carried away by a movement which the patient, absorbed in his ravings, did not realize, continued to repeat these letters and even to sign Achille's Christian name without him noticing it. It is generally known that such movements, accomplished in this manner without the knowledge of the person who seems to produce them, may be designated as automatic, and they were extremely numerous and varied in the case of this patient. Having noted this point I tried to produce these movements by mere command. Instead of speaking direct to the patient, who, as I well knew, would have replied with insults, I let him rave and rant as he pleased, while standing behind him I quietly ordered him to make certain movements. These were not executed, but to my great surprise the hand which held the pencil began to write rapidly on the paper in front of it and I read this little sentence which the patient had written without his knowledge, just as a few moments before he had unconsciously signed his name. The hand had written: "I won't." That seemed a reply to my order. I must evidently go on. "And why won't you?" said I quietly to him in the same tone; the hand replied immediately by writing: "Because I am stronger than you." "Who are you then?" "I am the devil." "Ah, very good, very good! Now we can talk!" It is not everyone who has had the chance of talking to a devil; I had to make the most of it. To force the devil to obey me I attacked him through the sentiment which has always been the darling sin of devils—vanity. "I don't believe in your power," said I, "nor shall I do so unless you give me a proof." "What proof?" replied the devil, using as always to reply to me the hand of Achille who suspected nothing. "Raise this poor man's left arm without him knowing it." Immediately Achille's left arm was raised. I then turned towards Achille, shook him to attract his attention, and pointed out to him that his left arm was raised. He was greatly surprised and had some difficulty in lowering it. "The demon has played me another trick," said he. That was true, but this time he had played the prank on my instructions. By the same procedure I made the devil execute a host of different actions, and he always obeyed me implicitly. He made Achille dance, put out his tongue, kiss a piece of paper, etc. I even told the devil, while Achille's mind was elsewhere, to show his victim some roses and prick his finger, whereupon Achille exclaimed because he saw before him a beautiful bunch of roses and cried out because he had had his fingers pricked. . . . Thanks to the foregoing method I was able to go further and do what the exorcists never thought of doing. I asked the demon to sleep in an armchair, and that completely, so that he should be unable to resist. I had already tried, but in vain, to hypnotize this patient by addressing him directly, and all efforts had been useless; but this time taking advantage of his absence of mind and speaking to the devil, I succeeded very easily.

Achille tried in vain to struggle against the sleep which overcame him, he fell heavily backwards and sank into a deep sleep. The devil did not know into what a trap I had lured him: poor Achille, whom he had sent to sleep for me, was now in my power. Very gently I induced him to answer me without waking, and I thus learnt a whole series of events unknown to everyone else, which Achille when awake in no way realized, and which threw an entirely new light on his malady. . . . In spite of the sleep in which Achille was apparently plunged he heard our questions and was able to reply: it was a somnambulistic state. This somnambulism, which had come on during our conversation with the devil and in consequence of a suggestion made to this latter is not at all surprising. During the course of his malady Achille had several times shown analogous conditions; by night and even by day he fell into strange states during which he seemed raving, and woke later retaining not the slightest memory of what he had done during these periods. . . . Achille . . . once put to sleep, was able to tell us a mass of details which previously he had not known or had known without understanding. In this state of somnambulism he related his illness to us in a manner completely different from heretofore. What he told us is very simple and can be summed up in a word: for the last six months he had had in his mind a long train of imaginings which unfolded more or less unconsciously by day as well as by night. After the manner of absent-minded people he used to tell himself a story, a long and lamentable story. But this reverie had assumed quite special characteristics in his weak mind and had had terrible consequences. In a word, his whole sickness was nothing but a dream. The beginning of the malady had been a grace misdeed which he had committed in the spring during his little journey. For a short time he had been too forgetful of his home and wife. . . . The memory of his wrong-doing had tormented him on his return and produced the depression and absence of mind which I have described. He was above all things anxious to hide his misadventure from his wife and this thought drove him to watch his lightest word. He believed at the end of a few days that he had forgotten his uneasiness, but it still persisted and it was this which hampered him when he wished to talk. There are weak-minded people who can do nothing by halves and constantly fall into curious exaggerations. I once knew a young woman who, wishing similarly to hide a fault, began to dissemble her thoughts and actions. But instead of dissembling on the one matter she was carried away to the point of hiding and garbling on everything, and began to lie continually from morning until night, even about the most insignificant things. In a sort of fit she let slip the confession of her fault, obtained pardon for it and completely ceased to lie. In the case of Achille it was the same thought of something to hide which produced this time not lying but complete mutism. It is already evident that the first stages of the malady are explained by the persistence of remorse and the fantasy which it occasioned. Already the anxieties, the day and night dreams, were growing more complicated. Achille overwhelmed himself with reproaches and expected to fall victim to all sorts of sufferings which would be no more than legitimate punishments. He dreamed of every possible physical disorder and all the most alarming sicknesses. It is these dreams of sickness which, half-ignored, produced the fatigue, thirst, breathlessness and other sufferings which the doctors and the patient had taken successively for diabetes and heart trouble. . . . Achille was always dreaming. Who has not had similar dreams and wept over his sad fate while watching his own funeral? These dreams are frequent with hysterical people who are often heard softly to murmur poetic lamentations such as: "Here are flowers . . . white flowers, they are going to make wreaths to lay on my little coffin," etc. Achille, sick and suggestible, went further; in spite of himself he realized the dreams and acted them. Thus we see him say farewell to his wife and child and lie down motionless. This more or less complete lethargy which lasted for two days was only an episode, a chapter in the long dream. When a man has dreamed that he is dead, what more can he dream? What will be the end of the story which Achille has told himself for the last six months? The end is very simple, it will be hell. While he was motionless as if dead, Achille, whom nothing now came to disturb, dreamed more than ever. He dreamt that, his death being an accomplished fact, the devil rose out of the pit and came to take him. The patient, who during somnambulism related his dreams to us, remembered perfectly the precise moment during which this deplorable event took place. It was towards eleven o'clock in the morning, a dog was barking in the courtyard at the time, disturbed no doubt by the stench of hell; flames filled the room, innumerable imps struck the poor wretch with whips and amused themselves by driving nails into his eyes, while through the lacerations in his body Satan took possession of his head and heart. It was too much for this weak mind; the normal personality with its memories, organization and character which had until then subsisted somehow, side by side with the invading dream, went under completely. The dream, until then subconscious, found no further resistance, grew and filled the whole mind. It developed sufficiently to form complete hallucinations and manifest itself by words and actions. Achille had a demonical laugh, uttered blasphemies, heard and saw devils, and was in a complete state of delirium. It is interesting to see how this delirium was constituted and how all the symptoms which it presents may be explained as consequences of the dream, as manifestations of psychological automatism and division of personality. The delirium is not solely the expression of the dream, which would constitute simple somnambulism with strictly consistent actions manifesting no disorder; it is formed by the mingling of the dream and the thought of the previous day, by the action and reaction of the one upon the other. Achille's mouth utters blasphemies, that is the dream itself; but Achille hears them, is indignant, attributes them to a devil lodged within him, this is the action of the normal consciousness and its interpretation. The devil then speaks to Achille and overwhelms him with threats, the patient's interpretation has enhanced the dream and sharpened its outlines.

If we wished to cure our unhappy Achille, it was completely useless to talk to him of hell, demons and death. Although he spoke of them incessantly, they were secondary things, psychologically accessory. Although the patient appeared possessed, his malady was not possession but the emotion of remorse. This was true of many possessed persons, the devil being for them merely the incarnation of their regrets, remorse, terrors and vices. It was Achille's remorse and the very memory of his wrong-doing which we had to make him forget. This is far from being an easy matter- forgetting is more difficult than is generally supposed.

In my work on the history of a fixed idea I have shown how this result might be approximately obtained by the process of "dissociation of ideas," and that of "substitution." An idea or memory may be considered as a system of images which can be destroyed by separating its constituents, altering them individually and substituting in the whole certain partial images for those previously existent. I cannot here repeat the examination of these processes, I merely recall that they were applied afresh to the fixed idea of this interesting patient. The memory of his transgression was transformed in all sorts of ways thanks to suggested hallucinations. Finally Achille's wife, evoked by a hallucination at the proper moment, came to grant complete pardon to her spouse, who was deserving rather of pity than of blame.

These modifications only took place during somnambulism, but they had a very remarkable reaction on the man's consciousness after awakening. He felt relieved, delivered from that inner power which deprived him of the full control of his sensations and ideas. The sensibility of the whole body was restored, he recovered the full use of his memory, and far more important, began to take an objective view of his ravings. At the end of only a few days he had made sufficient progress to laugh at his devil and himself explained his madness by saying that he had read too many story-books. At this period a curious fact must be noted: the delirium still persisted during the night. When asleep, Achille groaned and dreamt of the torments of hell: the devils made him climb a ladder which mounted indefinitely and at the top of which was placed a glass of water, or else still amused themselves by driving nails into his eyes. The delirium also existed in the subconscious writing where the devil boasted that he would soon reclaim his victim. These facts still show us therefore the last traces of the delirium which might persist without our knowledge. This should be carefully noted, for a patient abandoned at this point would before long fall back into the same divagations.

Thanks to analogous measures the last dreams were transformed and soon disappeared completely. . . . The patient no longer had the same complete forgetfulness after somnambulism nor was he now so deeply anaesthetic during the subconscious writing. In a word, after the disappearance of the fixed idea the unity of the mind was being reconstituted. Achille was soon completely cured. . . . It is pleasant to add that since his return to his little village the patient has often sent me news of himself and that for the last three years he has preserved the most perfect physical and moral health. (Oesterreich 1974, 110–117)

Comment: Janet ascribes the dramatic symptoms of this case to the exaggerated guilt and remorse of the patient (manifested in an idée fixe concerning his moral laxity) as well as a kind of irruption of the dream state into waking consciousness. This explanation, as far as it goes, seems correct but incomplete to me. I (and Freud) too see demonic possession as linked to guilt but Janet (and Freud) reduce all the symptoms to a personal guilt. I instead see the victim as taking on the guilt and crimes of the community in order to expiate through sacrifice the sins of the community. The cognitive content of the possession can sometimes be characterized as the irruption of dreaming cognition into waking consciousness. But again this cannot be the whole story. There is no reason to assume that the irruption of the dream state into waking consciousness should produce the kinds of symptoms this patient experienced. He apparently became quite depressed for a while and even catatonic for two days. Then he swung into a manic state and evidenced all the usual bizarre delusions of the manic state. In any case this patient fits our definition of demonic possession quite well. There was a transferral of agency to the demon so that the demon could speak while the patient had to stand helplessly by. The patient displayed the demonic behaviors in public and through the demon constantly accused himself of crimes and sins. The patient tried to destroy himself several times. Thus the patient fits the definition quite well. But then why did Janet's technique of hypnotic suggestion appear to work? The demon was eliminated via forgiveness of the patient. The patient's wife forgave the patient. Janet hypnotically and overtly delivered that message to the patient. Thus, the guilt motivating the need for a sacrificial victim was dissolved. Janet claims that the patient was well after three years of follow-up. If he had had a neurologic event or an episode of bipolar psychosis, the symptoms were bound to reoccur. They may not, however, have taken the form of demonic possession if the patient felt no need to embody, display, and destroy his own sins or the sins of the community.

Case 8

Here is a case from a traditional, premodern tribal culture, the Ba-Ronga.

I will now give full details of the case of Mboza, who was himself possessed at one time, and later on became a regular exorcist. After having worked in Kimberley for some time, he returned home in good health. But soon afterwards, he was lame for six months. He attributed his difficulty in walking to rheumatism (*shifambo*). There was some improvement in his condition, but he began to feel other symptoms: he lost his appetite and almost completely ceased to eat. Here is his testimony: "One day, having gone with another young man to gather juncus, in order to manufacture a mat, the psikwembu started at once in me" (*ndji sunguleka hi psikwembu psikaňwe*). I came back home, trembling in all my limbs. I entered the hut; but suddenly I arose to my feet and began to attack the people of the village; then I ran away, followed by my friends, who seized me and at once the spirits were scattered (*hangalaka*). When conscious again, I was told I had hurt a Khehla (a man with the wax crown . . .), and had struck other people on the back: "He!" said they, "he has the gods" (or he is sick from the gods, a *ni psikwembu*).

"In former times, the only remedy was waving a large palmleaf (*milala*) in front of the patient. This was deemed sufficient to 'scatter the spirits.' Now the treatment is much more complicated."[2] In the first place a medicine, the composition of which does not here concern us, is administered to the patient. After he has taken it, he must spit to the four quarters of the wind, pronouncing the sacred syllable *tson*, which has the power of moving spirits and begging life from them. Then a prayer is addressed to the gods.

In the hut, right in the centre, sits the patient. Melancholy, with downcast eyes and fixed glance; he is waiting. . . . Everyone in the district knows that to-day, this evening, when the new moon appears, the strange and terrible conjuration will take place. All who have ever been possessed are present. The master of the proceedings, the "gobela," whom the bones have designated, holds in his hands his tambourine, the skin of one of the great monitor lizards common among the hills, stretched on a circular wooden framework. In the beautifully calm evening air and as if to contrast hideously with the sun sinking in purple glory, the first tap resounds. It radiates, stretches on every side, travels through the thickets to the surrounding villages, and then there is sensation, an outburst of joy, made up of curiosity, malice, I know not what unconscious satisfaction. Everyone hastens up at this well-known sound, all hurry towards the hut of the possessed, and all desire to take part in this struggle, this struggle against the invisible world. Several persons are gathered there, some with their tambourines, some with great zinc drums picked up in the vicinity of the town . . . others with calabashes filled with small objects which are shaken and make a noise like rattles . . . and now, crowding round the patient, they begin to beat, brandish, and shake as violently as possible these various instruments of torture. Some graze the head and ears of the unhappy man. There is a frightful dun which lasts through the night, with short interruption, and until the performers in this fantastic concert are overcome by fatigue.

But this is only the orchestra, the accompaniment to which must be added, and it is of the greatest importance, singing, the human voice, the chorus of exorcists, a short refrain following a yet shorter solo, but which is repeated a hundred, nay a thousand times, always to the same end for which all work seriously and doggedly: that of forcing this spiritual being, this mysterious spirit which is present, to reveal himself, to make known his name . . . after which his evil influence will be exorcised. These chants are at one naïf and poetic. They are addressed to the spirit, extolling him, seeking to flatter him, to win him over, in order to gain from him the signal favour of giving himself up. Here is the first of those which I heard . . . one day when I was travelling and when, hearing a tremendous din behind the bushes, I jumped out of my wagon and fell into the very midst of a scene of exorcism: *Chibendjana! u vukela bantu!* (Rhinoceros, thou attackest men!) vociferated the singers around a poor woman who seemed lost in I know not what unconscious dream. My arrival hardly abated this infernal racket, notwithstanding the fact that the appearance of a white is generally an event in the villages of this district.

When hours pass by without any visible effect being produced on the patient, the refrain is changed. The night is perhaps far spent, the dawn is approaching. Come forth, spirit, or weep for thyself until the dawning. Why then are we evilly intreated? Or else by way of further emphasis, they go so far as to threaten the spirit that they will go away for good if he does not deign to accede to the objurations of these delirious drummers:

"Let us go away, bird of the chiefs! Let us go away. (Since you frown upon us)."

The melodies of these exorcists' incantations are of a particularly urgent, incisive, and penetrating character. This insistence is rewarded, the patient begins to give signs of assent. This means that the "Chikouembo" is preparing to "come out." The onlookers encourage him:

"Greeting, spirit! Come forth gently by very straight ways. . . That is to say: do not hurt the possessed, spare him!" Overcome at length by this noisy concert the possessed is worked up into a state of nervous tension. As a result of this prolonged suggestion, a fit, the hypnotic character of which is very evident, commences. He rises, and begins to dance frantically in the hut. The din redoubles. The spirit is begged to consent at last to speak his name. He cries a name, a Zulu name, that of a dead former chief such as Manoukoci or Mozila, the ancestors of Goungounyane; sometimes, strangely enough he utters the name of Goungounyane himself, although he is still alive . . . no doubt because the great Zulu chief is regarded as invested with divine power. A woman formerly possessed told me that she enunciated the word Pitlikeza, and it transpires that this Pitlikeza was a sort of Zulu bard who had wandered about the Delagoa country when she was still a girl. She was convinced that the soul of this individual had embodied itself in her, several decades after his passage through the district. In the case of the Mboza the patient was covered with a large piece of calico during all the drum performance. A first medicinal pellet was burnt under the calico, in a broken pot full of embers, a male pellet (made with the fat of an ox or a he-goat); no result having been obtained, a second pellet, a female one made from fat of a she-goat, was introduced. Nwatshulu prayed to the gods . . . .

When the second pellet was nearly all burnt, Mboza began to tremble; the women sang with louder voices. The gobela shouted amidst the uproar: "Come out, Ngoni!" Then he ordered the singers to keep quiet, entered under the veil and said: "You who dance, there, who are you? A Zulu? A Ndjao? Are you a hyena?" The patient nodded his head and answered: "No!" "Then you are a Zulu?" "Yes, I am . . ." And during a pause, he said: "I am Mboza." Mboza was a Ronga who died in Kimberley many years ago. The uproar was resumed and the third pellet was introduced. This was the "pellet par excellence," neither male nor female, the one which is expected to have the strongest effect. Mboza suddenly rose, threw himself on the assistants, beat them on the head, scattered them all right and left, and ran out of the hut feeling as if the spirits were beating him! "Everyone saw that day that I had terrible spirits in me." In the crisis of madness the patient sometimes throws himself into the fire and feels no hurt, or falls in catalepsy and strikes his head against wood, or the ground, without feeling pain.

But let us finish the description of the possessed man's fit. He dances, leaps wildly. Sometimes he flings himself into the fire and feels nothing, or else ends by falling rigid as if in catalepsy . . . his head striking against a block of wood or the earth, but he appears to feel no pain.

The concerted drumming may last for four days, a week, two weeks. I know a woman (who has now become a Christian under the name of Monika) who had to endure it for seven days. Everything depends on the nervous condition of the patient and the exhaustion produced in him by fast and suffering.

When the spirit has declared his name and title he is henceforth known and they may begin to question him. Spoon, the diviner, whose wife has been twice possessed, by the Zulus and the Ba-Ndjao, told me about one of these confabulations. He was in a neighboring village when suddenly messengers came to fetch him urgently saying: "Your wife, who was present at a witch-dance in such a place has been seized with the madness of the gods." He went to the place in all haste and saw that she was in fact out of her senses and was dancing like one possessed. He had never previously had any idea that she was possessed by a spirit. This spirit began to speak when she grew a little calmer, and replied to questions put to him: "I have entered into this ligodo, that is this body, this vessel, in such and such a way." "The husband had gone to work in the fold mines. I attached myself to him in a certain place when he was seated on a stone, and when he had returned to the house I forsook him to enter into his wife." "Are you alone, spirit?" is often asked. "No, I am there with my son and grandson," he will perhaps reply, or else if it is suspected that there are indeed several spirits with him those present continue to beat the drum to drive out the whole host. Sometimes the possessed pronounces as many as ten names. During this confabulation the spirit, speaking by the mouth of the sick man but remaining perfectly distinct from him, sometimes demands presents and there is one in particular which must be offered in order to satisfy and dismiss him. . . . Blood, blood in abundance is in fact necessary to effect the cure of the sick man and induce the noxious indweller to cease from harm.

Generally a she-goat is fetched if the sick person is a man, a he-goat if it is a woman. The exorcist who has presided over the whole cure returns and causes the onlookers to repeat the song which brought on the first fit. The possessed begins to grow excited and present the symptoms of raving madness which we have already described. Then the animal is stabbed in the side and he flings himself upon the wound, sucks, greedily swallows the flowing blood, and frantically fills his stomach with it. When he has drunk his fill the beast must be taken away by force. He must be given certain medicines (amongst others one called *ntchatche* which seems to be an emetic) and goes away behind the hut to vomit up all the blood which he has drunk. By this means, no doubt, the spirit or spirits have been satisfied and duly expelled.

The patient is then smeared with ochre. The animal's biliary duct is fastened into his hair, and he is bedecked with thongs made from the skin of the goat which has been cut up. These various ceremonies must symbolize the happiness and good fortune which the bloody sacrifice has secured for the sick man. All the drum-beaters, who are persons formerly possessed, arm themselves with these thongs also, crossing them over the chest in the ordinary way.

Does this mean that everything is now over? So violent a nervous attack, so complicated a series of disturbing ceremonies leave behind them a state of commotion and shock from which the possessed does not immediately recover. It appears that from time to time, in the evening, the bangoma, those who have passed through this initiation, are again seized with the characteristic madness and even sometimes strike their neighbours with the little axe which the Ba-Ronga use in their dances. By day they are in their right senses. This is not all; the fact that they have been in a special relationship with the spirits, the gods, confers upon them prestige and particular duties. They have themselves become gobela and may henceforth take part in the exorcism of the sick. They will perhaps earn money with their famous drums: this is why these ceremonies are in some sort an initiation; this is also why certain individuals are not sorry to be possessed and readily submit to the torture of the witches' Sabbath. (Oesterreich 1974, 139–143)

Comment: It is a remarkable fact that the essential ingredients of an exorcism ritual are the same in both "primitive," like the Ba-Ronga here, and modernized cultures. A person becomes ill and averse to the sacred. He is pronounced possessed (in this case on the basis of a divination procedure that involves throwing the dice). In order to heal the victim the exorcists learn the identity of the demon and then prepare a vessel or fetish object or sacrificial victim into which the demon is ritually transferred. Then the vessel is sealed away or destroyed. In this case the victim was healed by having the demon transferred to a sacrificial goat. Then the victim had to drink the blood of the goat in order to become one with the sacrificial substitute. Once he united himself with the substitute he could vomit out the substitute and get rid of the sins or impurities he had contracted.

Case 9

Perhaps the most famous case of demonic possession and exorcism is the case that the novel (and subsequent film) *The Exorcist* was based on. William Peter Blatty wrote both the book and the screenplay for *The Exorcist* based on a case of a Catholic exorcism of a teenage boy in 1949–1950. Apparently, a fair amount of the material depicted in the film was sensationalized but based on real events. The victim was a 13-year-old boy who started to experience paranormal phenomena after his aunt died. She had taught the boy to use a Ouija board to contact the spirit world. These "paranormal" events included unexplained noises, shaking and sliding furniture, and the sound of someone with squeaking shoes walking through the house. In the film after the possession became intense, bloody welts appeared on the victim's stomach as a message for help. Something like this apparently really occurred. The boy was evaluated at several hospitals with no clear diagnosis emerging. Like every other possessed person he had an aversion to sacred objects and imagery. The boy's voice changed and deepened, and he spoke as a demon emitting a stream of obscenities and blasphemies. Several Catholic priests and hospital staff witnessed the ritual exorcisms but it took over a month to cure the boy. Cure was signaled by the boy having a dream of an angel chasing the demons away.

Comment: It is difficult to evaluate the historical veracity of any of the details of the case. The victim is apparently still alive but has not shared anything about his experience. None of the people present at the exorcisms have presented detailed accounts of the case beyond the bare list of facts summarized here. If we assume that there is some truth in these facts then this case seems remarkably like all the other cases we have been considering in this chapter. There is a dramatic personality change involving a transfer of agency from the normal identity to a demonic identity. The demon hates the sacred and becomes violent and abusive in the presence of sacred things. The demon is also antisocial and self-destructive. There is a public display of demonic behaviors and destruction of the demon via ritual exorcism. The paranormal phenomena in this case, and in those of many other cases of demonic possession, are more difficult to explain. Enhanced cognitive capacities can be explained as the need to prove that the demon is supernatural and thus able to bear the sins of the community. I have no good explanation of paranormal phenomena however. The movie *The Exorcism of Emily Rose* (Boardman and Derrickson 2005) was based on the story of Anneliese Michel in Germany. This unfortunate girl died after she refused food and water and after dozens of attempts at exorcism had failed. By the theory I have propounded here, demonic possession is a form of self-sacrifice and if the demon cannot be destroyed, for one reason or another via ritual exorcism, then the victim will often try to destroy him- or herself via suicide. Demonic possession and exorcism are a deadly serious affair.

Consider now a couple of cases reported by Carrazana et al. (1999) where the neurologic background of the victim was studied.

Case 10

This 24-year-old Haitian man had his first generalized tonic-clonic seizure at the age of 17 years during the wake of an uncle. The patient had been sleep deprived during the vigil of the corpse. The seizure was attributed to possession by *Ogu* (the warrior god), the dead uncle's protecting *loa*. Subsequent seizures and morning myoclonus were explained as harassment by the wandering soul of the uncle. The possession was interpreted as a punishment, for the patient had been disrespectful toward the deceased in the past. He was treated by the local *mambo* (priest) for 6 years and did not see a physician until coming to the United States. His EEG showed 3- to 4-Hz bursts of generalized spike-wave complex discharges occurring spontaneously and during photic stimulation. In retrospect, the patient had a history of waking myoclonus, which had been ignored. He remained seizure free after treatment with valproic acid (VPA). The likely diagnosis is juvenile myoclonic epilepsy. (Carrazana et al. 1999, 239)

Comment: Once again, one of the causative factors of demonic possession is deemed to be guilt. As with Janet's patient described above this patient also had evidence of sleep and probably dream disorder. Both seizure and sleep disorders promote parasomnias or difficulty transitioning from one sleep state into another or from sleep to waking.

Case 11

This 36-year-old woman had several years of recurrent complex partial seizures that manifested as a strong sense of fear and epigastric coldness, followed by loss of awareness, utterances of nonsensical phrases, and complex motor automatisms. The local *mambo* attributed the events to her being taken by *"Melle Charlotte,"* a french *loa*, with the nonsensical speech being interpreted as a foreign language. It is said that during the possession by this spirit, a person will speak perfect French or other languages, even though in life, the person has no knowledge of that language. She continued to have seizures despite the *mambo*'s attempts to conjure the spirit. He explained his failure to the fact that *Melle Charlotte* is a very particular *loa* who makes only sporadic appearances. She was not treated with AEDs until she left Haiti at the age of 34. An EEG revealed a right anterior temporal focus, and magnetic resonance imaging (MRI) showed right hippocampal atrophy. Seizures improved with carbamazepine

(CBZ), although compliance with medication was a problem, largely because of family interference. (Carrazana et al. 1999, 240)

Comment: This case is particularly interesting as glossolalia was part of the clinical picture. Also we have localizing information: the EEG revealed a right anterior temporal focus. This is a site also implicated in hyperreligiosity (see McNamara 2009).

SUMMARY

The phenomenology of the possession experiences in the cases presented in this chapter is consistent: The possessed individual exhibits signs of unusual and persistent illness, immoral behaviors, motor tics, and nonsensical speech patterns. In all cases there is a reduction in agency and a transfer of agentic control over to the demonic entity. The demonic entity is, of course, antisocial, engages in taboo behaviors, and is generally averse to all that is sacred in the culture. He also displays extraordinary cognitive capacities and skills like precognition or what appear to be clairvoyant abilities. The demonic behaviors are witnessed by representatives of the community and a decision is made to destroy the demon via exorcism. The exorcism typically involves discovery of the identity of the demon. This ensures that the message the victim is trying to send about community sin is received and understood. Then a fetish object is ritually constructed in order to transfer the demon into that object which will be subsequently destroyed. Alternatively a sacrificial animal is ritually prepared and then the demon is transferred into the animal and the animal is destroyed. But most of the time the demon is simply expelled from the victim via the ritual exorcism and is in that way destroyed. The functional purpose of the possession is theorized to be to act as a scapegoat for the sins of the community. The victim is a sacrificial substitute for the community. The victim accumulates the impurities of the community until he is clearly demonic. Then the victim is sacrificed ritually by killing or expelling the demon. The sins of the community are thereby expiated.

In primeval times, during perhaps the Upper Paleolithic and the Neolithic the sacred or divine kings performed this sacrificial function for their communities. The king was in touch with all other persons in the community so he could accumulate all of the impurities and sins of the community into his person. At that point he was demonically possessed. He embodied the sins of the community. He was then ritually killed and a new king was installed. As kings gained greater political control over the course of millennia they managed to have human victims killed in their place. These substitutes would be treated like kings for a year during which time they could cumulate all the impurities of the community. Then they would be ritually killed. As human sacrifice came under criticism, animals were substituted for human victims. The animals chosen had to somehow plausibly carry the sins of the community. They needed to be ritually prepared and so forth. Priests were employed to perform these duties of preparing victims for sacrifice and ritual killings. Over time, however, the sacrificial rites of the priests began to lose their awe and people stopped reverencing them. At those times the sacred king had to step in and reconsecrate the realm usually via sacrificial rites of one kind or another.

People who become demonically possessed, I suggest, are willing victims of the sacrifice—not consciously of course. No one would consciously choose the suffering involved in demonic possession. Instead something about these individuals makes them suitable for carrying the sins of the community. In ancient times substitutes for kings had to be physically spotless. Kings themselves had to be physically beautiful without blemish. In modern times some other criteria besides physical health and beauty appear to operate when the choice is made concerning who will carry the sins of the community in order to expiate those sins ritually. No one knows what that distinguishing mark is, but it must index enormous physical and spiritual strength. How else could these people bear the awful suffering of demonic possession?

Chapter 5

Nightmares and Demonic Possession

Demonic possession has always been associated with changes in the dreaming patterns of the victim. For those at risk for possession or who become "infected" with demonic influences dreams begin to be experienced as unusually vivid, emotional, bizarre, and repulsive. Images of violence become more frequent. Nightmares, too, increase in frequency or become more horrifying. Demonic spirit beings, it appears, first manifest themselves in the dreams of their target victims. It is in the nightmare where the demon first attempts to take possession of the dreamer.

If one starts to awake from a nightmare, one may experience both a malignant presence in the room and/or a weight upon the chest that makes breathing difficult. For many people who experience this early awakening sleep paralysis state, the malignant presence is typically experienced as demonic. In this para-somniac state, one experiences the paralysis along with the respiratory distress typically associated with the REM sleep state all while one is in the process of waking up. Why one should also experience the sense of presence; a malignant presence is still unknown.

David Hufford (1982) has studied variants of sleep-related "spirit" phenomena. While a young man still in college, he himself had a vivid experience of being visited by a demonic presence during or after awakening from a nightmare. He heard the sound of his bedroom door creaking open and then footsteps moving toward his bed. He then felt an evil presence. He was aware of not being able to move. He became terrified. He next felt the demon on his chest restricting his breathing. He later told others that he felt he was going to die. Then suddenly the paralysis melted away and like many others who experience this nightmare, Hufford seized the moment to jump out of bed and rush to be with others and to not be alone with the terror.

Hufford began a scholarly investigation into his experience, which he found to be common. J. Allan Cheyne (1995) of the University of Waterloo in Canada has collected more than 28,000 tales of terrifying sleep-paralysis events. Cheyne runs a Web site (http://watarts.uwaterloo.ca/~acheyne/S_P.html) where visitors fill out surveys about their experiences during sleep paralysis. Hufford later reported that in the special cultures of Newfoundland and Nova Scotia the evil presence is conceived of as a hag or witch who targets young woman in order to prevent a pregnancy or to steal a soul.

In addition to the links between sleep-paralysis states and demonic infestation one also sees reports of religious specialists with experience in dealing with demonic possession who claim that they can predict who will become demonically possessed by examining the content of their own dreams after they are appropriately ritually prepared to receive these special dreams. Take, for example, this case from the well-documented Zar possession cult in North African cultures:

> She may have been warned in the course of her religious therapy that she is bothered by a rih al-ahmar, a red wind, or zar. . . . She might enlist the aid of a sitt al-'ilba—the "lady of the box," a reference to the tin which holds the spirits' incense. The sitt al-'ilba is a women known to have prophetic dreams and usually an adept of zar. During consultation she takes a bit of cloth that has been in contact with the patient's body, and a coin, some weeds, or perfume the latter has brought as gifts-items understood in the language of zar to be the "keys of dreams." . . . On retiring for the night, the practitioner burns some incense and while fumigating the objects, chants a zar thread that collectively invokes the spirits. Having thus linked her client to the world of zaryen, she places the objects beneath her pillow. When she wakes she informs her client whether she dreamt of spirits and if so what they desire in return for her rehabilitation—a sacrificial animal of a certain color, a ceremony of a certain length, a specific piece of clothing or jewelry. A woman's own dreams interpreted by those with knowledge of such matters might confirm possession diagnosis or alert her to impending spirit attack. A dream of henna, smoke, whiskey, chairs, a man or woman who suggests she wear a certain type of top, or anything else associated with zaryan, is a clear indication of possession. (Boddy 1989, 154)

Thus, both religious specialists in possession phenomena and nonspecialist, healthy, ordinary everyday people can be forewarned about impending demonic infestation or possession via their dreams. My interest here is uncovering clues as to the cognitive-emotional mechanisms involved in demonic possession. How does the old self/ego become submerged underneath that of the demonic personality? How is that submergence experienced by the individual? Can this process be reflected in dream content? If we take the dream ego to be an accurate reflection of the individual's emotional self then we might be able to document changes in subjective experience as a demonic possession event becomes imminent or unfolds. Of course we would need a consistent and longitudinal record of dreams reported by the same individual before, during, and after the possession experience in order to get a complete picture of the subjective experience of possession. I know, however, of no such dataset or collection of dreams.

An alternative to analyzing the longitudinal collection of dreams from a single individual undergoing possession might be to analyze a collection of nightmares from different individuals, none of whom report overt possession. If nightmares often involve "demonic infestations" of one kind or another, as the ancients believed, then one should be able to identify traces of those "infestations" in the content of the dreams themselves. If such content was found, then the links between nightmares and demonic possession would be supported. In addition, establishing such a link would allow us to study cognitive mechanisms of possession because we could track the variety of dream ego experiences with respect to different stages of the possession event or experience. More specifically we could plot out the process by which the demon supplants the dream ego as controller of the individual's mental states.

SELECTION OF NIGHTMARES WITH SPIRIT-POSSESSION THEMES

In a separate work on nightmares (McNamara 2008), I analyzed a collection of dreams that involved demon characters in the nightmare storyline. These nightmares were collected semirandomly from public Internet sites that archive dreams and nightmares posted by anonymous individuals. These people presumably wanted to share their dreams with others and perhaps get some feedback on their meaning. One of the most interesting things about nightmares is that people want to share them with others . . . as if they were red-hot memes itching to jump from one brain to another in order to replicate themselves as massively as possible. To select nightmares (with "demons" in them) for analysis, I simply searched Web sites for nightmares containing the word *demon*. I then randomly eliminated all but 15 such nightmares in order to keep this analysis at a manageable length.

The following caveats in the interpretation of these nightmares and standard explanations of the possession theme apply. I will be using shorthand when I refer to the word *demon* and when I ascribe intentional states to it. As scientists we have to assume that demons do not exist and do not exhibit intentional states. The characters and beings that populate dreams are accordingly products of the dreamer's own mind. So if we stick with this "standard" reductionist assumption, I believe that most psychologists, in order to explain dream characters like the demon, would subscribe to some sort of story like the following: The demon complex is a symbol or metaphor for some sort of underlying emotional threat. Some sort of psychic-emotional complex is surfacing in the unconscious of the dreamer and is experienced as an overwhelming threat to the psychic or cognitive integrity of the ego-complex or "self"-complex of the dreamer. In short, there is some internal memory or emotional storm that is threatening the psychic balance of the dreamer's identity or self. This is experienced by the dreamer as a threat of annihilation or worse. The threat is personified as an evil demon.

Whether or not we accept this sort of explanation for the dreams that follow below, it is clear that the dreamer within the dream, lets call him or her "the dream ego," is clearly feeling threatened by something that he or she considers "demonic." We, as scientists, can learn something about the ways in which mild forms of demonic infestation occur by examining these sorts of dreams/nightmares. When we put these data on demonic nightmares together with the testimony of premodern peoples considering dreams, nightmares, and demonic possession, it becomes clear that no account of demonic possession will ever be complete without an examination of the link between nightmares and demonic possession. Let us therefore proceed with this initial foray into an examination of potential links between nightmares and demonic possession.

Dream 1

Posted at the Nightmare Project Web site on September 14, 2001, by a 22-year-old female about a nightmare she had had when she was 16:

I dreamt that I could see myself sleeping. I lay on my left side in the middle of the bed, as I normally do when I fall asleep. It felt like an out-of-body experience more than a dream.

I started to hear a whispering at the foot of my bed. It sounded like an older man or demon whispering my name over and over again, very slowly.

I asked out loud, "Who's there?" Immediately, I was thrown off my bed by some very powerful force and started spinning around on the floor very, very rapidly. As I screamed as loud as I could, terrified, I looked up to see my ceiling fan spinning as fast as I was.

I woke up all of a sudden, but still in the position I had dreamt I was in. I turned on the lights and couldn't fall back to sleep for hours.

Comment: In this dream, the demon announces himself in a barely audible whisper. He also, by vocalizing the name of the dreamer, hints at his evil intention—to take over the identity of the dreamer. The dreamer, instead of trusting and allowing the demon into her consciousness, responds forcefully and demands to know "Who's there?" This demand to know the name of the demon (reminiscent of the procedures ritual exorcists had practiced thousands of years ago when they demanded to know the name of the demon they were confronting) apparently infuriates the demon, as the dreamer is thrown out of bed and spins around until she is awakened. Why should knowing the name of the demon protect the victim against the demon? It may be that knowing the name of the demon separates the victim's identity from the demon's identity and thus the victim is not totally possessed by or subjected to the demon.

In this case the dreamer is smart enough to demand the identity of the demon so she can separate herself from the demon's influence and control. We will see in the dreams that follow that the demon is allowed to get closer and closer to the ego of the dreamer and thus the danger of full scale possession by the demon increases accordingly.

Dream 2

The dream took place on the first landing of the stairs in the house we last lived in. It seemed that it was about 11 o'clock at night and pitch black. I was standing alone but I felt someone walking up the stairs behind me. Hard as I tried, I couldn't yell out or move as the person came closer. He came closer and closer but in the darkness I couldn't see who it was. As he reached for me I woke up shaking and in a cold sweat.

Comment: In this dream, a male, malicious presence is close to but not identical with the dreamer. No possession of identity has yet taken place. This sort of dream, being chased by a malicious being who is close while we are powerless, is so common as to be a stereotype—but the malicious presence in this case carries with it a demonic edge as the dreamer had to wake up in order to forestall possession or destruction by the intruder. From a straightforward phenomenologic perspective the demon has gotten close to the dreamer so he has the power to paralyze the dreamer's ability and even will to shake off the intruder.

Dream 3

Posted to the Nightmare Project Web site February 24, 2000, by a 29-year-old male about a nightmare he had had when he was 18 years old.

I used to live in a peculiarly-shaped apartment, not the kind everyone thinks of. My bed faced a closet, large and dark, with huge wooden doors.

As I dreamt one night, a demon burst through the apartment door, and called me by a name I do not go by, but still I recognized it as mine. When the demon saw that I recognized this name, his already demonic appearance grew far more evil, and he let out the most blood-curdling roar I have ever heard. The demon chased me around the apartment, and cornered me in my bedroom. I jumped in bed, under the blankets, knowing for some reason that this was a safe zone.

The demon came into the room and waited in the closet for me to get out of bed. It tired of waiting, and let out another horrifying scream. It scared me so badly that I woke up, lying in my bed, staring at the closet. The door was half-open, as the demon had left it. The feeling of pure evil was still so real, I was positive the demon was in the closet. I was petrified until daylight. To this day, it still makes me wonder.

Comment: In this dream the demon is already very close to possessing its victim because the demon knows the name of the victim—apparently the real name of the victim. The dreamer recognizes the peril he is in and flees. He finds a safe zone that allows him to exclude or prevent the demon's influence over him. But the demon tires of waiting and prepares to possess the dreamer. The dreamer has to wake up to prevent the catastrophe but even after waking he still palpably feels the presence of evil in the room. Phenomenologically speaking the important point here is that there is a way to prevent the demon from hurting the dreamer. Initially it is finding a safe zone or some part of the mind that is off limits to the demon. The demon will respond by attempting to invoke fear in the dreamer. Often this will work but in this case it apparently did not work.

Dream 4

Posted at the Nightmare Project Web site on September 02, 2000, by a 19-year-old female who had had the nightmare a year earlier:

This dream made a huge impact on me. It involves my mother, to whom I am incredibly close.

She and I were in a very small town when we found a cave. We, along with everyone else in the town, decided to explore it together. In the cave we found two demons, each with the body of a goat and the head of a dog, and cloven feet and hands. At random, they started ripping out and eating the hearts of the townsfolk. Some of the victims died. Some didn't.

Then the demons escorted us out of the cave and into the sun. At this point, they turned into beautiful women with long, black hair and blood-red lips. They asked my mom and me to take them somewhere in our car, and got into the back seat. My mom looked at me over the top of the car and said, "One of us has to survive this."

Those were her last words. I did not see the demon women rip out my mother's heart, but it was understood.

Comment: A psychoanalytic interpretation of this nightmare would likely claim that the dreamer wished harm to the mother but this would miss the essential action of the nightmare: the mother's self-sacrificial act on behalf of her daughter. The mother apparently sacrificed herself so that her daughter would survive the attack of the demons. Since the nightmare is the dream of the daughter and not the mother, the demons are there to possess the dreamer, not the mother or the townsfolk. This dream demonstrates that the demons can appear in beautiful and appealing guises. They do not necessarily have to appear as hideous. Indeed they may be more dangerous to the dreamer in proportion to their true nature being hidden. The dreamer in this case was protected against possession by the demons via the intervention of her mother.

Dream 5

In the following nightmare from Barb Sanders, a woman who donated a huge corpus of her dreams to the eminent dream researcher Dill Domhoff in California, the dreamer sometimes comments on many images in her dreams and these comments help us to understand the images from the point of view of the dreamer (not necessarily the waking "Barb

Sanders"). This point of view (the dreamer's) is precisely the perspective we need to get a valid first-person phenomenological picture of the themes in the dream/nightmare. I will therefore first print the nightmare report here in its entirety so that the reader can get the gist of the narrative. I will then comment on individual themes to bring out the richness of the report for our analyses on the possession theme in nightmares.

From the Dreambank.net Web site, January 6, 1981

A nightmare. Entities or souls or creatures from other planets are coming to meld with humans and take our spirits away. I am very frightened. The children are the first to go and then the adults. It's a terrible feeling of the fear of losing myself as through death or absorption into another. They come, 3 of them. The one coming for me is a big man in a chicken hawk suit with red and blue fluffy feathers. He talks like an English pirate (irate)? We meld and a transparent form of my body is tucked under his wing and off we fly. What a ride. I can feel my stomach lurch as we go zipping up to the cosmos and down again. It's like a jet plane. We get to their planet. Then a man gets shot and falls. I'm surprised because I thought, "1.) No one dies here, and 2.) ugly, mean people don't exist here." They take the body of a 2 yr old baby and this shot man's soul goes into the baby. His face, is only softened and rounded like a baby. I'm appalled because they had told me we were just being borrowed. Now I know we were being lied to. I feel awful. I tell Nate to run. "I'm sorry I got you into this mess."

Now I will reprint here individual themes of the nightmare and comment on them accordingly.

Entities or souls or creatures from other planets are coming to meld with humans and take our spirits away. I am very frightened.

The dreamer here explicitly states that possession of the identity of the dreamer is the aim of the demons: they want control of the minds of humans. Barb Sanders tells us what it is like to lose one's identity to a malicious presence: "It's a terrible feeling of the fear of losing myself as through death or absorption into another."

At first the demon appears in a farcical form of a chicken-hawk suit:

We meld and a transparent form of my body is tucked under his wing and off we fly.

Sander's identity is melded into that of the demons. Note that the dreamer's identity is not lost here. There is a melding or fusion of the two. So complete possession has not yet occurred. Instead the dreamer seems to not to take the threat seriously anymore. She senses that the threat is empty.

But then things rapidly become bizarre, gruesome, and horrifying.:

They take the body of a 2 yr old baby and this shot man's soul goes into the baby.

The sacrificial use and slaughter of innocents recalls the ancient cults involving infant sacrifice and modern tragedies like that of Otty Sanchez mentioned in a previous chapter.

Dream 6

We will see in the next nightmare (another one from Barb Sanders) an elaboration of the theme of trusting "demons" and then regretting it. Once again I will first reprint the nightmare in full and then comment on several subthemes in the nightmare.

From the Dreambank.net Web site, September 9, 1981:

A frightening dream. I went to a party. Everyone is drinking, laughing, and frenetic. I hesitate to join them. They swirl around me, encouraging me to join them. Darryl sits across from me. He teases me and says something about a girl he used to know. I feel the same old distance from him (placed by him). I call him Howard and feel embarrassed. A lot of people disappear. The party seems to have moved on down the street, maybe to Aunt Elaine's house. I belatedly want to join them now. I drink some wine. I feel slightly high. Instead, I end up in my living room. An Uncle and a cousin are there. I greet them. I laugh at my cousin because he carries a rifle on his shoulder everywhere he goes. I say, "How silly, you are getting carried away." A man then appears at the door. He's smiling gently and wants me to join the party. I feel a desire and a fear to go. There is some danger to me if I go. I clutch my cousin and say, "Look at my hand. See the bullet wounds?" He looks. He says, "There is poison here, you've been poisoned." The man beckons me to come to the party. I realize then that they've gotten their poison into me, but not quite enough. I still can resist. I say, "I don't want to be a part of your project." It is hard for me to say because the drug makes me want to go. I say it several times and he just stands there waiting for me, because he knows the drug is powerful. I'll be sucked into another being like in the invasion of the body snatchers. I run to my "dad" and plead with him, telling him I don't want to, and to please help! I'm trying to but I'm growing weaker. "Please help me!" He doesn't respond to me other than to weakly smile at me to acknowledge that he has heard me. I grab my cousin, who before I had seen as weak and silly and cling to him, hugging him hard, hanging on like he was my anchor to that room. Then a fat lady, mostly naked is dancing at a party. Her husband picks her up off the floor and makes love to her. He is detached, fully clothed, and his back is to me. She is fully exposed. I see her vagina. I see her face clearly. A prim blonde woman sits rigidly beside them. I am shocked. This is on T.V. After he's done, the man sticks a fat piece of paper in the blonde woman's mouth. She is disgusted. It's a symbol of a large penis. Her red lipstick forms an "o" around it. Then I am upstairs in my bedroom. I wake up from a nightmare. I run downstairs, crying, "The little men are inside my stomach!" I'm crying. My Uncle or grandfather soothes me. He says, "No, it isn't possible. I've been barricading the stairs for you all night." I am not comforted. I go back upstairs. I sit on the bed and hug my nanny. She is an old square robot, and not very sophisticated. I ask it, "Why aren't there any nice men for me?" It says, "Look, there are," and shows me two of them (on a screen on its chest). I say, "But if I take them, what will be left for my brother!" Nanny laughs and shows me many women for Dwight. I am still worried. Then I'm at a dance, watching the musicians. One can't find his banjo. Then he finds it and sees that something has eroded the outside. I realize that what ever "they" touch, corrodes like that and that "they" are there. I turn and the man is standing there, smiling. He says, "It's so close. We almost had you." I try to resist.

The dreamer uses various tricks and maneuvers to avoid possession by the demons in this dream. The demons tell her in no uncertain terms that "we almost had you." To the extent that the dreamer and the demons represent two different entities in the dream the danger of full possession resulting in a single demonic identity remains a danger rather than an accomplished fact.

A lot of people disappear. The party seems to have moved on down the street, maybe to Aunt Elaine's house. I belatedly want to join them now. I drink some wine. I feel slightly high. Instead, I end up in my living room. An Uncle and a cousin are there. I greet them. I laugh at my cousin because he carries a rifle on his shoulder every-where he goes. I say, "How silly, you are getting carried away."

The dreamer loses some of her ability to evade capture and possession as she drinks some wine and her judgment becomes impaired. She wants to trust "them" but something in her calls up from memory some protective force against "them"—her cousin. Her cousin apparently was not a very trusting guy. He was not so gullible. Yet the dreamer wants to let "them" in so she denigrates the cousin who carries around a rifle on his shoulder—presumably to deal with threats.

A man then appears at the door. He's smiling gently and wants me to join the party. I feel a desire and a fear to go. There is some danger to me if I go.

The demons appear friendly in order to seduce the dreamer into joining with them. But, the dreamer, finally senses danger.

I clutch my cousin and say, "Look at my hand. See the bullet wounds?" He looks. He says, "There is poison here, you've been poisoned."

Now the dreamer fully realizes that she has been infiltrated . . . some poison has seeped in via a wound. The "silly" but now reliable cousin is the source of her information and strength at this point.

The man beckons me to come to the party. I realize then that they've gotten their poison into me, but not quite enough. I still can resist. I say, "I don't want to be a part of your project."

This is the decisive moment of the nightmare. The dreamer struggles to reject the fusion attempt with the aliens/demons.

It is hard for me to say because the drug makes me want to go. I say it several times and he just stands there waiting for me, because he knows the drug is powerful. I'll be sucked into another being like in the invasion of the body snatchers.

The demons do not give up easily. They rely on the power of the drug/poison. The dreamer needs to call in more help.

I run to my "dad" and plead with him, telling him I don't want to, and to please help! I'm trying to but I'm growing weaker. "Please help me!" He doesn't respond to me other than to weakly smile at me to acknowledge that he has heard me.

She turns to foundational sources for her identity but they are weak at best.

I grab my cousin, who before I had seen as weak and silly and cling to him, hugging him hard, hanging on like he was my anchor to that room.

She returns to the cousin who has displayed strength in the past. But now the demons put on more pressure. Things become more bizarre, horrifying and grotesque.

Then a fat lady, mostly naked is dancing at a party. Her husband picks her up off the floor and makes love to her. He is detached, fully clothed, and his back is to me. She is fully exposed. I see her vagina. I see her face clearly. A prim blonde woman sits rigidly beside them. I am shocked. This is on T.V. After he's done, the man sticks a fat piece of paper in the blonde woman's mouth. She is disgusted. It's a symbol of a large penis. Her red lipstick forms an "o" around it.

Now the dreamer is shown the full consequences of an alliance with, or fusion with the demons. There will be degradation and a loss of self unless help comes from some source.

Then I am upstairs in my bedroom. I wake up from a nightmare.

Here we have a dream within a dream. The possession theme is often associated with these sorts of amazing switches in consciousness during a dream. The dreamer thinks she wakes up but is not really awakened. If the dreamer believes that she has awakened, then she becomes more trusting and more easily "poisoned" or controlled.

I run downstairs, crying, "The little men are inside my stomach!" I'm crying. My Uncle or grandfather soothes me. He says, "No, it isn't possible. I've been barricading the stairs for you all night."

The demons want to persuade the dreamer that the threat is gone. That she is now safe.

I am not comforted. I go back upstairs. I sit on the bed and hug my nanny. She is an old square robot, and not very sophisticated. I ask it, "Why aren't there any nice men for me?" It says, "Look, there are," and shows me two of them (on a screen on its chest). I say, "But if I take them, what will be left for my brother!" Nanny laughs and shows me many women for Dwight.

As the dreamer struggles to protect her identity, the bizarreness levels of the images increase. She once again attempts to draw upon old foundational persons relevant to her identity, in this case a nanny. The nanny, like all the other characters in the dream, except crucially the cousin, tries to convince her that the danger has passed.

I am still worried.

The nanny's ploy does not work. The dreamer remains concerned and therefore vigilant.

Then I'm at a dance, watching the musicians. One can't find his banjo. Then he finds it and sees that something has eroded the outside.

The dreamer finds herself at another festive event and then finds more evidence of the infiltration of the demons . . . a musical instrument has been touched by them and has been damaged.

I realize that what ever "they" touch, corrodes like that and that "they" are there. I turn and the man is standing there, smiling. He says, "It's so close. We almost had you."

This is a fascinating turn of events in the dream as the demons come right out and admit that they are trying to possess her, the dreamer . . . and almost succeeded! Will the dreamer now let down her guard?

I try to resist.

The fight is not over and the dreamer continues to resist. All forms of guile and trickery have not managed to persuade the dreamer to let down her guard and let the demons in. They will need to mount a more violent attack in situations like this.

Dream 7

Posted at the Nightmares Project Web site on August 6, 2000, by a 38-year-old female who was 14 when she first had this nightmare:

It would start out as a fairly ordinary nightmare (I suffered frequent nightmares in my youth). Generally some demonic, evil thing would be chasing me, or some such scenario. Knowing at some level that it was a bad dream, I would try my best to wake up from it by calling out or making some sound. Finally, after much effort, I would wake up screaming.

My sister, to whom I have always been extraordinarily close, would then enter the room to comfort and console me. She would embrace me and pat my back, and tell me that I was all right, that it was only a dream.

But, just as I would calm down, with my heart and breathing gradually returning to normal, my sister would suddenly break away from me. Leveling me with a piercing, evil stare, she would slowly back away and begin laughing in a cruel, maniacal way. I would then realize that I had not woken up at all, that it was a false awakening. In reality I was still dreaming, still in the nightmare, not yet released from my frightening night-visions. Again, more desperately now, I would struggle and struggle in a vain effort to awake while my dream-sister continued to cackle.

Then I would suddenly awake, sweating and screaming. My dear sister would rush to my side, only to back away again and laugh. . . .

This loop might be repeated four or five times before I would actually wake up. Of course, when my sister truly came to comfort me when the episode really *did* end, I would be nearly hysterical with fear, not trusting that she was actually my true sister!

Comment: Here we have several of the themes we covered when discussing Barb Sander's nightmares. In order to annihilate the identity of the dreamer and to possess that person, the alien identity needs to gain entrance into the trust of the dreamer. Thus the alien identity will take on the form of a trusted person familiar to the dreamer. The dreamer then relaxes his defenses against possession and therefore the dreamer can be infused with the poison of the demons and thus made more weak and tractable. The demons also use various tricks to fool the dreamer or to lull the dreamer into a false sense of security. In the above dream we also have the phenomenon of awakening from a dream within a dream. Once again we see that the demons use this as a ploy to gain the trust of the dreamer—to make her believe that she is now safe. In this case the aim appears to have been to drive a wedge of fear and distrust between the dreamer and her "dear sister." Presumably the sister was a foundational source for the dreamer's identity and had to be undermined in order to gain control of the dreamer's identity.

Dream 8

In the next dream the dreamer allowed demonic influences in to her trust via a drug experience. In volume 1 of this work I reviewed several historical instances of ecstatic possession cults that turned destructive once drugs or intoxicants of some kind entered the picture.

Posted to the Nightmare Project Web site March 25, 2000, by a 15-year-old female who was 14 at the time she had the nightmare.

I went to my room and shut the door in order to get away from my family. My walls are normally light blue, but in the dream they were white and the light from the window shone so perfectly as I lay down on top of my bed. The radio was playing a song that went, "I'm going out for awhile so I can get high with my friends, don't wait up 'cause I won't be home." I felt peaceful and content as I closed my eyes.

I felt my body begin to float, which didn't bother me until I realized that I couldn't get down and had lost control. Suddenly I heard a demon's voice, and as I looked in the mirror across from my bed I saw a devil-like creature. I was still floating, but now thought I would fall. I frantically tried to get down. Hearing this demon's voice frightened me so much I began to pray for help from God, but found I couldn't speak. I kept trying, but I couldn't get up enough breath. Finally, I managed to get out the words, "Help me, help me." I fell back onto my bed, and right then I woke up.

Comment: Once the demon gains entrance into the trust of the dreamer, possession follows quickly and with possession, the dreamer loses agency. This dramatic loss of agency, of will and identity, is vividly described in this dream. It feels like weightlessness; not being rooted in the earth. When she looked in a mirror the dreamer saw herself as already possessed by a demon. She then realized her acute danger and she called for help. The call succeeded.

Dream 9

In the next nightmare no such happy ending occurs.

Posted at the Nightmare Project Website on May 27, 2000, by a 42-year-old female about a nightmare she had when she was 28 years old.

I had this dream while in graduate school. I was walking back to my dormitory on a winter night, just after sunset. The street lamps bathed the scene in an orange light. Suddenly, a thick, pea-soup, London-type fog descended. Unable to see at all, people froze in place. For me, that was the corner of my dorm and the main street. People called to each other trying to get their bearings. Among them, I heard some friends. I called out to them, "I'm in front of Henry Hall. If you follow my voice, you can get home."

"Okay," they responded.

And then, just as I knew my friends were approaching, I began to change into a hideous monster. I could feel my fangs and claws growing, and was sure my eyes were turning red. I felt demonic, and knew that as soon as my friends found me, I would kill them.

I have dreamt of turning into a monster or demon many times.

Comment: One feels that this dreamer may have already succumbed to the demons as she experiences the dream from the point of view of the demon . . . the one who wants to consume identities. She uses guile to gain people's trust and then she "knows" that she will kill them. On the other hand perhaps this dreamer is particularly powerful and able to resist possession by an "alien" being/character. In that case her experiences would be invaluable as she could get into the mind of the agent attempting to destroy others. This is the kind of person who would have become a candidate sorcerer or shaman in premodern societies.

Dream 10

In the next dream the dreamer attempts to resist the loss of his identity to the demons but seems to partially fail as he was just a child when the assault came.

Posted at the Nightmare Project Website on September 10, 2001, by a 27-year-old male about a nightmare he had when he was 8.

One stormy night, I was wakened by thunder and went to my parents' bed. After I went back to sleep, I had this dream.

I am wearing a mask depicting the face of a demon. Naturally, I remove it, but behind it is another demon mask, and behind that another. I can never get all the masks off my face.

I awoke in a cold sweat. Hanging on the wall of the bedroom were the masks I had worn in the dream. Needless to say, I woke up my parents.

Comment: Perhaps the dreamer's parents found a way to protect the true identity of the dreamer as he apparently psychically survived the attack when he was just a child. His strategy of physically tearing off the false identity is a good one but a difficult one for a child as there is no strong identity yet in place that can replace the false one.

Once the demon makes the attempt to take over the identity of the dreamer the dreamer must respond—either fight back or lose out to the demon. Losing out to the demon means increased vulnerability to daytime psychopathology. So a fight is recommended. But how do you fight "them"? This quick look at the content of nightmares reported by apparently average people suggests many strategies to resist loss of autonomy and agency as well as catastrophic loss of identity and possession by some other alien entity experienced as demonic. We have seen that some dreamers, particularly children, know how to find a safe zone in their minds. They can hide there for a while. Other individuals, adults, can use their memories to call up trusted characters or personages to help them in their struggles with the "demons." Yet other more religious dreamers can call upon God for help; this strategy seems to be particularly effective even for nonbelievers.

EXPLANATIONS OF DEMONIC POSSESSION THEMES IN NIGHTMARES

In all of these nightmares we have a dreamer who is experiencing a terrifying threat—a threat not just of annihilation but of take over and control by some other entity. The threatening entity is experienced as demonic. Its aim is to possess and control the dreamer and to do harm to the dreamer and to others. While other types of nightmares contain themes of aggression, terror, and violence, they do not typically contain themes of loss of autonomy, or of control and enslavement by some alien entity bent on harming the dreamer and others. What causes these sorts of "possession-themed nightmares"? We have seen that the standard account of nightmares simply cannot do justice to the richness of the cognitive content in these possession dreams. The standard account of nightmares is that they represent a failure to integrate painful affect or memory contents into long-term memory systems. But this standard theory cannot account for possession-themed nightmares. Not every nightmare sufferer has an emotional memory or trauma that threatens the ego integrity of the dreamer. In possession-themed nightmares, the dreamer's ego identity system seems to be under threat. But this is not the case with most nightmares, and it is hard to see how inability to integrate painful memories into long-term memory should existentially threaten the ego identify of the dreamer. Even if we assume that emotional trauma is present in a nightmare sufferer, it is not clear why it has to be symbolized with a demon. Why not some other symbol of threat? There are millions of threats out there. Many are not considered "evil." Instead they are considered dangerous but dumb. What is interesting about possession-themed nightmares that cause distress is that they have characters in them (demons) that *intend* to take over the identity of the dreamer and then to do the dreamer harm. Yet the dreamer knows very little more about the evil demon than this bare fact. The dreamer's ability to read the mind of the evil demon starts and stops with his ability to understand that the demon intends overwhelming harm to the dreamer's essence, not just to the dreamer's physical body. It is odd, furthermore, to claim that the demon (or any other character in a dreamer's dreams except for the dreamer himself) represents some other part of the dreamer's mind because that would suggest that one part of the mind "wants" to take over control of the "self" part of the mind. But why should this be? If the demon was part of the dreamer's ego to begin with then presumably it already is in possession of the dreamer's mind/personality so there is no need for it to attempt to take over the personality/mind of the dreamer. Yet that is manifestly precisely what it intends to do.

Analyzing hundreds of nightmares exposes a pattern in the demon-possession themed nightmare. The demon apparently patiently works to take over control of the dreamer's mind and personality and uses cunning, guile, seductive wish-fulfillment images, and finally outright violence to do so. The demon announces himself first in a barely discernable voice or via a barely discernable touch or a barely discernable but ominous presence in the dream. Then the demon may attack individuals who are important to the dreamer in waking life; family members and such. Once the demon gets "close" to the dream-ego and obtains some sort of trust from the dreamer, an attack ensues. The demon will brave a short, swift, spasmodic attack on the dreamer often in the form of a small animal or some other small creature that attacks the dreamer. The dreamer realizes that this attack is serious even though the creatures are small and relatively easy to deal with. Next the demon will take on more formidable forms like large animals, space aliens, zombies, or actual demons and now the dreamer runs for it. The demon gives chase and may or may not catch the dreamer. Eventually the dreamer allows the demon to get close to him in the dream. The demon usually accomplishes this by tricking the dreamer. The demon pretends to be someone whom the dreamer trusts. By the time the dreamer realizes the mortal danger he is in, the demon has succeeded in getting a kind of spiritual or emotional hold on the spirit of the dreamer and thus the dreamer is especially vulnerable in these dreams/nightmares.

Eventually, the demon makes a full-scale attempt to take over the identity of the dreamer. This attempt may occur in a hundred different ways depending on the personal idiosyncrasies of the dreamer. The common denominator in these nightmares is that the dreamer becomes unsure of his or her identity and the experience is unwelcome and terrifying. Note that there are some individuals who enjoy playing around with identities in their fantasies and dreams and these people are not in danger of "possession" of dissociative disorder. In nightmares, on the other hand, the sudden loss of identity is frightening and deeply disturbing to the dreamer. Once the demon makes the attempt to take over the identity of the dreamer the dreamer must respond—either fight back or lose out to the demon.

If demonic possession fundamentally concerns replacement of a true identity with a demonic identity, then how does this phenomenology account fit with the social-historical account of the possession theme we have provided in this work? From a historical point of view demonic possession appears to occur when the sacred kingship is weak. When the kingship is weak the sacrificial system that normally eliminates impurities (due to sin and transgression) no longer does so. The impurities then accumulate. They do so first in vulnerable individuals. The most vulnerable are women, and so women are more likely to evidence demonic possession in these historical circumstances. From the point of view of the at-risk individual the accumulation of impurities is indexed by guilt (this was Freud's signal contribution). Guilt in turn would then be symbolized as a threat to the ego integrity of the individual and this situation would first manifest in dreams. As the level of guilt increases (due to the historical situation) so the level of threat would increase in the dreams. Note that individual elimination of guilt (via confession for example) would only help temporarily as unless the social situation improved the impurities would simply start to accumulate again. Society's transgressions have to be handled by the social system one way or another. Up until the modern era they were handled either by the shamans or the sacred kingship. It is not clear how the sins of our lives are handled today.

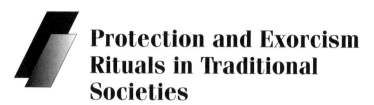

Chapter 6

Protection and Exorcism Rituals in Traditional Societies

Did the earliest human beings, our ancestors of the Middle and Upper Paleo-lithic, believe in demons? Did they develop rituals to protect against evil spirits? Did the Neanderthals believe in evil spirits? We will probably never know for sure. As discussed in volume 1 of this work it seems probable that both Neanderthals and our direct ancestors of the Middle and Upper Paleolithic believed in spirits. They probably both had developed theory of mind abilities—after all, even some great apes evidence some abilities to read the intentions of their conspecifics. In addition both Neanderthals and anatomically modern humans (AMH) in the Middle and Paleolithic periods buried their dead. There are figurines dating to these periods of therianthropes, half-human, half-animal beings that appear to indicate a shamanic worldview wherein one would become possessed by the spirit of the animal in order to perform healing or to be successful on the hunt. There are hundreds of such figures painted on the cave walls as well.

ETHNOGRAPHY OF DEMONIC POSSESSION
IN TRADITIONAL SOCIETIES

If we turn to the evidence from the ethnographic records of traditional peoples who live lives that are broadly similar to the lives led by our ancestors, it again seems probable that our ancestors believed not only in spirit beings but in malevolent spirit beings that could possess, harm, and even destroy people.

Take, for example, the masked dances of the Tibetan lamas. These were discussed in volume 1 and they are often intended to exorcise evil spirits

or to ward off harm. Tibetan Buddhism retains a good deal of the shaman-
istic ritual practices and beliefs of the people of the Eurasian steppes and
the highlands near the Himalayas. Among the Chokwe (Bastin 1984), a
matrilineal Bantu people of northeastern Angola between the Kwango and
Kasai rivers, ancestral and nature spirits are called the *Mahamba* (singular:
hamba). These are represented by trees, pieces of termite mounds, intention-
ally simplified figurines, and by masks. Some are malevolent spirit beings
or become malevolent if religious duties are neglected or purity regulations are transgressed. An angry hamba may cause infertility in women
and illness in men and women. Malevolent spirits also haunt the forest and
the bush laying wait to possess a passerby. If possessed, a religious specialist can perform an exorcism using various means to get the evil spirit to
leave the body of the ill person and enter into a fetish object like a ritually
prepared piece of clothing, a figurine, or a mask. If someone should touch
these fetish objects into which an evil spirit has been banished/captured
and imprisoned, that person may in turn become possessed.

To perform an exorcism, that is, to transfer or banish the evil spirit and
capture it in a fetish object, the religious specialist must first conjure the
evil spirit causing the illness. For that purpose the exorcist uses some sort
of divination procedure or instrument, one of the most widespread being
the *ngombo ya cisuka*, a round basket containing 60 small symbolic objects.
The *tahi* (exorcist or doctor) shakes the basket, and the subsequent pattern reveals the cause of the illness, usually a hamba spirit that the tahi
specifically names. Note that this is remarkably similar to the exorcism
procedures used by the ancient peoples of the Near East, including Jesus
himself. The exorcist first needs to discover the identity of the demon, his
name, and then use royal authority to command the demon to leave the
host and enter into some other object, such as the desert, a herd of pigs,
and so on. After the identity or name of the spirit has been discovered a
cimbanda or individual who had suffered from the same spirit in the past
is called to assist. He rubs the patient with medicine made from plants and
clay, particularly the purifying white clay (*pemba*), which symbolizes innocence. The evil hamba leaves through the patient's mouth and into a fetish
object, usually a mask or figurine, which becomes the exorcised spirit's
prison. After the purification, the cimbanda initiates the patient into the
cult of that evil spirit. An animal is sacrificed, its blood sprinkled on the
fetish object. The animal is then cooked and eaten and the fetish object is
placed in a shrine at the patient's house.

Note the use of a divination procedure and bowl to identify the evil
spirit afflicting the patient. Mayan Kings and rulers also used divination
bowls and mirrors to call up gods and to initiate sacrificial rites.

In China *Shigong* dance masks were used in ritual dances to appease the gods, while *nuo* dance masks protected from evil spirits. Interestingly masks play a role in warding off evil in Bali as well. Some monstrous-looking masks called the *Kirtimukhas*, "Visages of Glory," are believed to protect against evil. Among the Baga and Nalu peoples of Ghana, demons are personified in masks, heads, or animal figurines called the *as a-tshol* (among the Baga Sitemu), *ielek* (among the Baga Fore or Buluhfits), or *ma-tshol* (among the Nalu) (Curtis and Sarro 1997). Among the Baga, a-tshol/lek heads are kept by each lineage in the "big house," where ritual objects are stored and some lineage ceremonies are conducted. These heads/masks and ritual objects are said to offer protection against many forms of evil (especially sorcery).

In Nigeria, one protects against demons by imprisoning a witch in a sealed house where pepper is burning (Isichei 1988). These peoples put suspected witches through all kinds of physical ordeals designed to prove their guilt, including poisoning her, imprisonment, banishment, and so forth. If found guilty, the witch could be executed or sold into slavery. Enlightened colonial administrators outlawed these practices against suspected witches but the people bitterly resented this legislation. Women especially were outraged at this enlightened legislation as their fertility depended on protection against witches. The people attributed all kinds of natural and political disasters that followed the legislation to the inability to restrain the evil practices of the witches.

In Yourubaland in Nigeria demonic possessions often are believed to be caused by witches. The main protection against demonic possession is to become a member of a secret society. The Egungun and Oro, secret male cults, include among their many activities the identification and killing of witches. Most of the time, however, witches can be neutralized and evil spirits mollified via ritual masking and dancing. "We dance to appease our mothers," "mothers" referring to the witches. It is interesting that the myths of these tribes link the protection against witches and demonic possession to the strength (or weakness thereof) of the sacred kingship. Nupe tradition, for example, explains the origin of the royal masquerade, Ndaka Gboya, as the invention of a king whose government was weakened by his mother's interference. The mask swallowed the mother and then became a fetish object for a secret male society that identified and killed witches.

Among the Indian tribes of North America the Iroquois religious beliefs regarding demonic spirits have been studied. Interestingly, like the Yoruba in Africa they too have secret male societies (called the False Face Society) who use masks as fetish objects to protect against witches and demons. As in Africa one of the functions of the secret male society is to identify and neutralize witches—though it is not clear that they actually killed witches. Demons and witches are thought to cause all kinds of illnesses and it is sometimes difficult to separate rituals for exorcism from rituals to cure the ill. The curative rite of the Onondaga Iroquois False Face Society involves assembly of Society members at the sick person's bedside. The blowing of ashes from the hands of the masked dancers onto the ill person's head initiated spirit possession and healing. Members wearing masks (who are considered spirit beings when wearing the masks) lifted the ill person, while reciting prayers. Then a feast was shared by all.

In another rite, one designed to protect against evil spirits before a possession could occur, False Face Society members travelled about the reservation visiting the private homes. They danced a dance in each home that was designed to expel demons from the homes. They purged the home of evil and malevolence by rubbing large turtle shell rattles against the furniture, walls, and floor of the home.

A major winter ritual used by the Salish peoples of British Columbia and Washington state was called the spirit dance. A person with an illness, thought to be caused by possession by an evil spirit, would undergo a process of initiation into the dance ritual. The shaman would oversee all aspects of the ritual including preparation of the "patient" and the dance itself. He would teach the initiant the dance and urge her or him to find his own spirit song. The candidate was secluded in a longhouse ceremonial building while relatives and other tribespeople sung songs outside, drummed, and paid reverence to the candidate's spirit totem, thus increasing the spiritual power attributed to the being. That being had the power to expel the evil spirit. The shaman put the candidate through a series of grueling tests while the people outside danced their spirit dances. Many of them were former patients who had recovered and were now displaying their spirit powers. Many wore masks and acted as the spirit beings. Once the candidate had found his own song he appeared in public and was given a new mask and costume. The spirit was in the mask and could therefore be controlled. Thus, these possession cults were not ecstatic. Instead they benefited the community directly through healings and displays of social solidarity.

PROTECTION RITUALS

We have seen that the basic procedure for ridding a person of a demon has been to identify the demon and then to command it to enter some other object like a fetish object that was ritually prepared to imprison the demon.

People everywhere, including people in traditional societies, have also developed myriad ways to protect against demonic infestation or possession in the first place. Ethiopian Christians will generally carry an amulet or talisman, known as a *kitab*, or will invoke God's name, to ward off the ill effects of an evil spirit (*buda*).

In the ancient Near East people buried incantation bowls in the foundations of their homes to protect against infestation by evil spirits. These were small pottery bowls that were inscribed with magical texts or verses that would repel demons trying to enter the homes.

In almost every culture studied, bells were believed to be potent weapons against demonic infestation. So too sacred incense or sacred smoke of all kinds including tobacco smoke could protect against demons. Salt was considered protective. Holy water was and is considered a very powerful protective as is holy scripture, prayer, ritual gestures of various kinds, and the company of holy people.

Traditional peoples believed that demons could infiltrate into the mind and body of a victim through the malevolent intervention or machinations of a witch or via a transgression of some kind or even via accidentally touching a fetish object like a mask that contained an imprisoned demon.

Other routes of infestation were mirrors. Mirrors were considered a kind of portal to another reversed world where demons held sway. The Mayan kings used mirrors to conjure gods of all kinds. Incense was burned before a mirror and the king then "read" the images in the mirror through the smoky haze.

Mirrors could also steal one's soul. When a person looks into a mirror who does that person see? Him- or herself? But the self is the one who is looking—not the one in the mirror. So who is the one in the mirror? If one saw oneself in a mirror in a room where a death just occurred it meant that that person was to die soon as well. Mirrors were fundamentally evil because they *doubled* things.

Traugott Oesterreich, in his massive work on possession (1922/1974), describes a phenomenon referred to as *Verdoppelungserlebnis* (doubling of consciousness) in which the individual really experiences a double awareness of two forms of cognitive content, each from the same identity, and then two separate identities during spirit possession. In the first phase of this doubling effect, the individual can get the uncanny experience of the doubling of cognitive aspects of the self as well as doubling of the entire self concept; this experience is known as the experience of the double. The experience of meeting one's own double (the doppelganger) has been reported throughout recorded history and has most often been described in literature as a profound and dangerous encounter with a demon.

In neurology, experience of the double is treated as identical to or related to the phenomenon of autoscopy (seeing one's self). Autoscopy is a hallucinatory perception of one's own body image projected into external visual space. In both psychiatric and neurologic syndromes, the double usually appears suddenly, directly in front and about an arm's length away from the subject. It is virtually always a frightening experience. Most frequently only the upper torso (face and shoulders) of the double can be seen. As the subject raises his or her right arm the double will raise its left, and so on. The image is usually not seen in color. These facts point to a projection of a *memory* image (the only place the subject ever sees a mirror image of him or herself is in the mirror!) rather than a new or constructed image.

Regardless of the route by which a demon infiltrated the souls of its victims, whether it be through transgressions, touching impure fetish objects, or being captured by the double image in a mirror or being the victim of a witch, infestations could be prevented by constant vigilance, repeated ritual purifications, and outright exorcisms when necessary. The ancient Romans for example, celebrated a festival in May called the Lemuria. The festival was designed to be a community-wide purification event. The head of each Roman household washed his hands three times, placed black beans in his mouth, and walked barefoot through the house, tossing beans over his shoulder and chanting, "With these beans I do redeem me and mine." The chant was repeated nine times and the chanter could not look back. The demons would take the beans and depart.

The theme that emerges from this brief survey of protection from demonic infestation among traditional peoples is that demonic influences were considered impurities and could make a person physically sick. The first line of defense against infestation and possession was repeated rituals of purification. The next line of defense involved all kinds of magical protections from incantation bowls placed in the foundation of homes to the wearing of protective amulets on one's person. Despite all these precautions, impurities could be acquired in myriad ways including from female witches. Once impurities accumulated and could not be gotten rid of in the usual way, then special exorcism rituals had to be conducted. The general strategy in an exorcism ritual was to identify the evil spirit. Prepare a prison (e.g., a fetish mask or figurine) for that spirit. Command it to leave the patient and enter the fetish. Ritually seal the prison and either put it in a shrine or destroy it or bury it away from the village. All of these practices by traditional peoples were probably also practiced by our ancestors of the Middle and Upper Paleolithic to a greater or lesser degree. All of these practices certainly survive, as we will see, in one form or another in the traditions that lead to the Western world.

Chapter 7

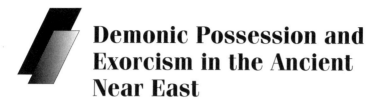

Demonic Possession and Exorcism in the Ancient Near East

In this chapter I trace the development of ideas and practices concerning demonic possession and ritual exorcism in the cultures that directly influenced the Western religious tradition. When examining these ancient religious systems one theme that emerges consistently and largely across cultures is that demonic possession was tightly linked with religious purity concepts and regulations. The demonically possessed were those who were unclean or impure or who had transgressed the purity laws in some way. As discussed in volume 1 of this work purity regulations operated on the idea that an individual and a people accumulated over time impurities that needed to be periodically eliminated. Impurities came from myriad sources but one of the root impurities had to do with menstruation. Women undergoing their "period," as we call it nowadays, were required to purify themselves and to avoid contact with others. Contact between a man and a woman during her period was strictly forbidden. Presumably the idea behind this strange prohibition was not mere hatred of the female sex but rather that blood indicated injury, illness, and death. Anthropologists have pointed out that menstruation is an evolutionary puzzle. Humans and some of their close cousins—the great apes—are the only mammals that exhibit overt blood flow during the fertility cycle. Why is that? There are as of yet no clear answers to this question. Whatever the reasons for the overt blood flow, it is clear that the flow would be used and interpreted as a piece of vital information concerning the fertility of the sender. Once the blood flow became a signal both senders and receivers of that signal would then develop behaviors around that signal in order to negotiate reproductive behaviors. Males competed for access to fertile women and fertile women had to find ways to regulate that access in order to select the best men. The standard theory on purity laws and menstrual taboos in particular (e.g., the taboo against contact with a woman during her period because men would become unclean if they saw or touched a woman during the blood flow) is that oppressive male political coalitions instituted the purity laws to control women. But this idea seems implausible as the purity laws appear to have been supported by women themselves because they protected women from unwanted attentions of coercive males.

Whatever the ultimate origins and functions of purity laws, it is clear that human societies needed a way to regenerate or become pure after a long period of impurity. The purity regulations kept a community relatively clean or pure but they were never really adequate by themselves. Therefore many cultures developed the so-called scapegoat mechanism whereby the community's impurities were poured into a special receptacle and then the receptacle was destroyed. When that receptacle was an animal or human being, the victim was ritually sacrificed or driven away from the community. Then the community was considered born again and pure. The sacred king was for many centuries considered responsible for collecting up the impurities of a community and then finding a way to eliminate those impurities through some sort of sacrificial or scapegoat mechanism. When the kingship operated effectively evil was effectively eliminated from the community via the sacrificial system. When the kingship was not operating effectively the sacrificial system began to break down and people became more vulnerable to cumulating impurities. Some of these people were then considered demonically possessed.

AFFLICTION AND DEMONIC POSSESSION IN ANCIENT EGYPT

Ancient Egyptians developed a variety of techniques to protect against demonic possession. The possession experience in ancient Egypt seems to involve transformation of both mind and body of the possessed. Oesterreich cites an inscription found at Thebes that described a demonic possession of a woman named Bint-Reschid, sister to the queen of Bachtan. The king of Egypt sent a priest, a man "who knows all things," to cure the girl. He examined her and determined that the exorcism would require a transfer of power or virtue from the god "tranquil in his perfection" to the possessed girl. The god (presumably his statue or fetish object) was brought into the presence of the girl, the priest then recited the necessary incantations, and the transfer of virtue was accomplished. The girl was cured. Apparently devotees of the god of Serapis were chosen by the god via a dream. After the dream they would be possessed by the god and then compelled to stay in the temple precincts serving the god until they had another dream liberating them from the god. The possession was often felt as a kind of affliction that the devotee ardently wished to end.

Egyptian priests followed strict purity regulations. Special priests, the wa'ebs, performed purifying rituals over objects to be used in the sacrifice. A priest had to purify his whole body with water and natron before performing the sacrifice. This was done in ritual baths within the temple precinct. He then put on clean, white linen (wool was considered as unclean as it came from live beings and could transfer impurity). Contact with women was forbidden for several days before the priest could perform special sacrifices.

THE CONDEMNATION OF DEMONIC ALLIANCES IN ANCIENT ZOROASTRIANISM

As recounted in volume 1 Zoroaster began his reforms of the pre-existing Indo-aryan religious system sometime between 1000 and 650 BCE. We have seen that Zoroastrianism was one of the first religions to identify the evil deeds of human beings with individual choice that is influenced by morally evil demonic spirit beings. To protect against the influence of demonic spirits the Zoroastrian recited the creed (Fravarane), professing to reject the company of the evil Daevas, and the Lie. If an individual chose the company of evil spirits these spirits then began to possess that person. The alliance of the individual with the Lie would turn that individual into a receptacle for the Lie. Like virtually all other ancient religious systems the Zoroastrians tended to equate sin and impurity or pollution. As with virtually all other religious systems these impurities included contact with ritually unclean things such as a corpse or a woman experiencing the menstrual bleeding. Impurities could be eliminated in most religious systems via the sacrifice (in primeval times the sacrifice was the king himself). In Zoroastrianism, however, Zoroaster had identified the Soma sacrifice as partially corrupted and in need of reformation. In the Soma ritual, a ritually prepared hallucinogenic drink was consumed and then animals were sacrificed. All too often however the rituals would spiral out of control due to the hallucinogenic effects of the Soma mushroom drink. Participants would become intoxicated and then act in very dis-inhbited and aggressive ways to anyone nearby. If the participants were warriors they would raid neighboring villages or communities while intoxicated with Soma. Zoroaster eliminated these outrages by regulating the Soma ritual and by prohibiting violence. Zoroaster's reforms, however, made the sacrificial system itself questionable. Zoroastrians, therefore needed something in addition to the sacrificial system (once reformed) to eliminate impurities. Exorcism became that additional ritual that could effectively eliminate impurities. The exorcism ritual appears to have consisted of chanting aloud the Ahuna-Vairya "The will of the Lord is the law of righteousness . . .," performing the (reformed) Soma sacrifice (described in volume 1 of this work) and reciting the Fravarane. One could also recite the twenty names of Ahura mazda.

The purity laws observed by Zoroastrians are described most thoroughly in the sacred texts. Fire and water are clean but the dead and dying are unclean—except for the animals killed in the blood sacrifice. Anything issuing from the body is unclean—even semen during the sexual act. Purification must follow directly after the act. The extent of the purity regulations regarding bodily effluvia is amazing. Even hair clippings after a haircut need to be put in a special fetish bundle, deposited ritually in the forest, and then covered with special dust and then left. Menstruating women must undergo some of the most elaborate purification rituals known to religion called the barasnom.

DEMONIC AFFLICTION IN ANCIENT MESOPOTAMIAN CULTURES

The asipu was the physician/priest/sorcerer who generally performed exorcisms in the ancient Near Eastern cultures of Mesopotamia (Assyria, Sumeria, Akkadian, and Babylonian cultures). He had some professional or official religious status as he was connected to the local temple cult. The kassaptu was a female witch who conjured up malicious demons in order to harm others. The kassapu was a male sorcerer but he was a much less feared or less common presence than the female witch. The divination specialist or priest was the Baru. According to the ancient Surpu handbook of exorcism (written in cuneiform and dating to about 1500 BCE), the asipu believed that people became possessed by demonic beings via sins/transgressions or via a kassaptu curing the person or via the maliciousness of the demons themselves. The individual in this case was just unlucky. The Surpu ritual exorcism was performed when the possessed individual did not know by what act/transgression he had offended the gods and therefore been afflicted by a evil spirit. The ritual itself consisted of chants, prayers, incantations, and the burning of various ritual items after the patient had handled them. There appears to have been an explicit demand that the patient perform a symbolic act in order to be exorcized. If he and the evil spirit had transgressed, then that act needed to be undone so the patient had to ritually unpeel or undo an onion or a piece of matting or a twine of goat's hair etc; these objects were thrown into a fire to be burned. If an individual was possessed by the Ahhazu demon ("who comes up from the ground") the evil spirit is transferred from the patient to the "Ninkilim, lord of the animals" who then would transfer the evil spirit to the vermin of the earth. Just as the sacred king was treated as a scapegoat figure in the ancient world such that he was able to collect up all the transgression of the people and then eliminate them sacrificially, so too the primeval shaman would call up the master of the animals in order to facilitate the hunt or a cure and so forth. Here again in the context of the ancient Near East the master of the animals was still the key to the well-being of the people.

The Udug-hul ("evil demons") handbook of procedures for ritual cures due to demonic afflictions was written in Old Akkadian and dates to about 2300 BCE but contains some tablets that date to about 300 BCE. In other words the collections preserve some 2000 years of practices. Interestingly demonic possession per se where the demon takes up residence in the mind/body of the patient is only rarely described in the Udug-hul. Instead the demon is depicted as covering or afflicting the individual like a cancer or skin disease. The text seems more concerned with identifying the demons who afflict individuals rather than how the demons afflict. One tablet (5) refers to seven demons known as the "watchmen." One wonders if there are connections here to the references to the fallen angels called the "Watchers" in the Hebrew scriptures. The incantation priest in the Udud-hul commands the demon to depart from the patient and threatens the demon with divine wrath if he does not obey. There are many incantations that serve to protect the priest/exorcist from contamination by the evil spirits. So what we have in the Udud-hul is the exorcist able to protect himself against the demons, lists of names of demons to be used against the demons themselves, and a commanding presence in the person of the priest. All of these elements of an exorcism will be found again among the early Christians and in the New Testament scriptures.

The procedures for cures or in some places for what appear to be ritual exorcisms described in the Udud-hul appear to have involved a ritual cup (the ansam-cup filled with water and tamarisk) and the innus-plant. The patient would drink this concoction while incense burned in a censer and the exorcist recited incantations.

In the collection of texts known as the Maqlu ("Burning") we have a series of incantations designed to protect against witchcraft. The "patient" is thought to be afflicted due to malicious magic emanating from a witch. The asipu's role is to act as the patient's advocate before a series of divine beings. The asipu contends that his patient has been slandered or hexed by a witch and her demons. The asipu pleads the patient's case before the night court of Anu, the netherworld god Ereskigal, the sky god Enlil, the chthonic god Ekur, and finally the sun god Samas and the subterranean gods Ea and Asaluhj. The witch is present in the ritual in effigy form. After the incantations are completed the asipu somehow divines whether the case has been made and the gods have granted a release from the bewitchment. Presumably the effigy of the witch was burned in that case—an eerie precursor to the burnings of witches in the premodern era in Europe.

The role of the Baru is different from the role of the asipu. The Baru is the diviner. He served the sacred kings and the military. These specialists appear to have preserved some of the ancient knowledge (derived from the shamans) of control over spirit-possession experiences. The Baru could conjure a spirit being but avoid the uncontrolled possession state. He could read the future by conjuring a spirit via inspection of the liver of a sacrificed sheep or by casting oil on water or by noting patterns in the smoke rising up from a censer. The Native American shamans and the kings of pre-Columbian Meso-American cultures also used the technique of "libanomancy" (divination via observation of sacred smoke). The Baru sometimes worked collaboratively with other specialists such as the dream priest—the *sa'-i-li*. All of these religious specialists worked effectively against possession or affliction by evil spirits and all can be found in the Hebrew scriptures as well.

Ritual purity regulations were ubiquitous throughout the Near East in the ancient world. Uncleanness or ritual impurity resulted from contact with menstruating women, with illness, with physical deformity, death, madness, or with any clear transgression of a religious law. Exorcisms were one technique used to make the unclean clean again. A demonically possessed person could be sprinkled with blood from a ritually sacrificed piglet or, as we have seen, fumigation with everything from sulfur to specially prepared incense could also eliminate a demon from a person and make him or her clean again.

EXORCISM AND TREATMENT OF THE POSSESSED IN ANCIENT GREECE

We learn in the *Odyssey* that after Odysseus avenged his honor by killing the suitors who had invaded his home and harassed the faithful Penelope, the home and household had become ritually impure due to all the killing and bloodshed and due presumably to the suitors' sins. Thus the house had to be made ritually clean again via fumigation with sulfur.

Thus, like all other ancient peoples the ancient Greeks lived in a world of purity regulations. Their ideas about demonic possession however were not derived solely from the idea of ritual impurity.

The ancient Greeks believed in daimones, minor deities and maleficent spirit beings that could possess people. The Greek tragedians often refer to madness as possession by a god like Dionysus or Eros, or daimon such as Pan or Hecate. The alastor is an avenging spirit that drives its victims to right a wrong committed elsewhere, but often tragedy results. The Erinyes are more often depicted as malicious demons out to hound to death and punish a transgressor. The Greeks produced some profound reflections on the Sacred Disease, epilepsy, in a tractate of that name dated to the fifth century BCE. This treatise explicitly denies possession as a primary cause of epilepsy. On the other hand, for many other less-complex maladies people were often advised to go to a temple like the temples dedicated to the god Asclepius. Asclepius would cure via a dream. Like other ancient cultures of the ancient world the ancient Greeks practiced purification rituals that could eliminate evil influences thought to cause possession and sickness. *Miasma* was the term used to indicate defilement due to contact for example with a menstruating women while the term *Agos* was used to refer to a tainted individual who had defiled himself by committing a sacrilegious act. To deal with cases of miasma and agos individuals had to perform the proper sacrifices and libations and then act to purify themselves from alastores. Various methods were used to attain purification including transfer of the power of the daimon out of the individual and into a fetish object or statue of some kind. The object would then be placed in a forest or some other remote location. The public ritual of the pharmakos operated on similar principles of transfer of impurity from the individual or community onto a scapegoat that then could be eliminated. Like the person of the sacred king, the pharmakos was an individual who accumulated all the impurities of the community. The individual in question (in Athens it was two men) had to exhibit some physical defilement. He was then treated like a king at the city's expense but then he was either killed outright or beaten with clubs and driven away from the city. Similar scapegoat rituals are reported around the world but usually they involve the sacred king.

DEMONIC AFFLICTION AND POSSESSION
IN ANCIENT ISRAEL

The ritual purity laws of ancient Judaism are found in Leviticus 13–15. Like all other ancient Near East cultures the ancient Hebrews found disease, death, and bodily effluvia ritually unclean. Thus, the menstruating woman (Niddah), semen, blood, and contact with corpses were all considered impure. People with these impurities were ostracized from the towns and not allowed to enter the Temple in Jerusalem. A woman with menstrual blood flow was not allowed to touch anyone until her menstruation was over. To become clean people had to wash their hands in ritual waters or to bathe in a ritual mikvah with full immersion. It is not clear that the ancient Jews considered the ritually impure as demonic. It was not until the intertestamental period that ritual impurity began to be equated to the demonic, for example in some of the Dead Sea Scrolls and among the Essenes at Quram.

There is very little explicit description of demonic possession in the canonical scriptures comprising the Hebrew Bible. Nevertheless, there is abundant material in those scriptures that alludes to demonic forces, afflictions, and possessions, and how to deal with those forces. We have seen in volume 1 that possession by the divine spirit of Yahweh himself was described in the Hebrew scriptures and when it occurred (e.g., Num. 11:17, 20–30; Deut. 34:9; Judg. 144:19; 1 Samuel 10, 16, 19; 1 Kings 3:28; 2 Kings 3), it invariably meant that the possessed individual was eligible for the leadership or sacred kingship. Like the sa'-i-li, dream-priests of the Mesopotamian sacred kings, Joseph and Daniel of the Hebrew scriptures have the ability to interpret dreams and do so at some foreign royal court. Like many other ritual practices dream interpretation as depicted in the Hebrew Bible appears to function to purify the sacred King. Joseph's and Daniel's dream interpretations refer to afflictions or dangers that the sacred king and his kingdom will undergo unless compensatory actions are initiated. There are other sorts of religious specialists in the Hebrew scriptures as well, such as the Witch of Endor who specializes in conjuring the spirits, prophets who do battle with evil chthonic deities, the goddesses of ecstatic fertility cults, magicians who provide various forms of services, and so forth. In addition to the appearances of these sorts of religious specialists throughout the Hebrew scriptures, Yahweh himself is depicted as engaged in a battle with evil spiritual beings that afflict humankind. These evil spirits carry names like Leviathan, Behemoth, Satan, Rahab, Chemosh, and several others besides.

It is worth pausing here and describing the so-called Watcher tradition in the Western experience with demons as it originates in the Hebrew Bible and then informs the entire demonic possession tradition in the West. The Watchers are mentioned in Genesis 6. They were created by God to watch over humankind, instruct them in the arts and sciences, praise of God and generally promote their well-being. Instead these angelic beings, when they beheld the beauty of womankind, began to lust after them.

They took human form and had sex with (possibly raped) the women. The offspring of these unions were giants called the Nephilim. The children of these Nephilim, in turn, were demons who tormented humankind. These are the demons that are responsible for most possessions in the Western tradition. One of the demons, Asmodeus, mentioned in the Hebrew scriptures (in the Book of Tobit 3:8) is of Zoroastrian origin. The name derives from *aesma daeva* (Demon of wrath and lust). Asmodeus went on to have an extensive history of possessions down through the centuries. In Tobit Asmodeus lusted after Sarah and killed, one after another, her seven husbands. Yahweh sent Raphael to help Sarah defeat Asmodeus. Raphael taught Tobias, Sarah's last husband, to grind the heart and liver of a glanos fish, then burn it as incense. The incense would drive away the demon. This ritual worked. But Asmodeus still acts to wreck marriages and incite lust and wrath. The lore around Asmodeus represents him as one of the fallen Angels, who, like the Watchers, lusted after mortal women and to whom were born the Nephilim. From the non-canonical (except in the Orthodox Ethiopian church) Book of Enoch (third century BCE), we learn that after the Watchers became corrupted, and they along with their offspring began to corrupt the human race, God decided to destroy them all in a great flood. He had the uncorrupted Watchers/angels bind the corrupted Watchers. There were 200 corrupted angels. They and their myriad followers were defeated and bound. They called to the seer/prophet Enoch to intercede for them with God. He advised them to sing a liturgy to God begging forgiveness.

We cannot leave this brief discussion of demonic possession among the ancient Jews without mentioning the mezuzah. These are biblical verses from Deut. 6:4–19 and 11:13–20, inscribed on deer parchment at a specified sacred time when angelic and astral influences were optimal and attached to doorposts of houses to protect against demons. While the tradition dates back to ancient Israel the attribution of protection against demons stems primarily from the Middle Ages. In orthodox circles similar protective "amulets" called the Tefillin and the Tsitsith may be worn on the head and attached to the garment respectively.

With these this all-too-brief discussions of ancient Near East and Greek religious ideas concerning demonic possession, we are ready to consider the main source of the Western tradition concerning demonic possession—the Christian tradition.

Chapter 8

Demonic Possession in Early Christianity

Out of all the world religions, I do not believe there is any more prone to see existence itself as a battle between good and evil than Christianity. Even the Zoroastrian religion, the originators of the good and evil warfare view of history, was not as dedicated to the good and evil distinction as the Christian religion because the Zoroastrians never developed as dramatic a history of demonic possession phenomena as did the Christian tradition in the West. The Eastern Christian tradition, of course, also saw the world in terms of a battle of good and evil but they too never developed a history of periodic eruptions of ecstatic demonic cults with all the destructive consequences that follows from these eruptions, as did the Christianity of the West. Ecstatic demonic cults probably never took off in the East (e.g., in the Byzantine empire) because the Eastern forms of Christianity retained the idea of the divine or sacred kingship in much more robust, strong and consistent ways than did the West. Thus to really understand demonic possession phenomena we would do well to focus on its history in the Western Christian tradition.

We will see that the peculiarity of the West is that the sacred kingship was always weak relative to polities across the rest of the world. The two cultures that most informed the Western tradition in Europe were Greece and Rome—the birthplace of democracy and republicanism respectively. Like the ancient Hebrews (the third source of the Western tradition) both of these cultures initially rejected the sacred kingship in favor of democracy or republicanism. Both projects failed miserably and thus both cultures attempted to reinstate the sacred kingship but failed again at that project. In Rome Julius Caesar was assassinated before we could accept the kingship from the citizens of Rome. In Greece the kings of Sparta defeated the

Athenian democracy but could not translate that victory into a restoration of the kingship in Athens before the Macedonian kings conquered all of Greece and then the world. Socrates and Plato recommended the development of the philosopher kings but Socrates was executed and Plato's message would not be appreciated in the West until the era of Charlemagne. Of course, we now know that democracy and republicanism never last and could not last in either Greece or Rome. That is because democracy and its milder variant, republicanism, always give rise to tyranny. Inevitably there is a response to the tyranny in the form of a universalizing empire that acts to put down the rule of the mob once and for all. I know of only a single instance where this sequence has not occurred: Switzerland.

In any case how do demonic possession phenomena fit into the special history of the West? As I just argued I think that that demonic possession really came into its own in the West and that is because it had no opposing forces. There was no strong sacred kingship to oppose the demonic or ecstatic cults. Instead there was a theology of good and evil that promoted the idea of a potent evil as constitutive of identity and reality. When the king is weak the priests grow stronger. They in turn have an interest in advertising, if not promoting, ecstatic cults because these chaotic phenomena justifies the peculiar priestly vocation—the performance of the sacrifice and the enforcement of purity regulations. Of course, if chaos and disorder became too extreme the priests were out of a job as well, so the priestly interest was in the toleration of just enough disorder to justify the continuation of the sacrificial rites but not too much disorder to create unmanageable amounts of chaos. In the absence of the kingship, society cannot effectively eliminate impurities so they accumulate within individuals. Those who become possessed are those who cannot bear too much guilt or impurity. To correct for the absence of the sacred kingship, the priesthood has to work overtime to eliminate the stain of transgressions and impurities from the society. Sacrificial rites therefore become more bloody and more frequent, and the priesthood grows in strength politically.

A similar historical configuration of a weak kingship and a strong priesthood occurred in the pre-Columbian cultures of Meso-America virtually throughout their thousand-year history. No king became strong enough for long enough to prevent disorder, so the priests stepped into the vacuum and began the spectacular and prodigious orgies of human blood sacrifice that stains the history of that region.

Interestingly, the West was given a fair chance of developing a strong sacred kingship because a core theological message of early Christianity was an endorsement of the sacred kingship. But just when the West was ready to accept this redeeming Christian message concerning the sacred kingship of Christ, the emperor Constantine transferred the capital of the empire from Rome in the West to Constantinople in the East. The Eastern rite Christianities embraced the core Christian message of the sacred kingship but the West did not. The primary reason the West never really received the core message of Christianity (i.e., the divine kingship of Christ) is because there was no strong kingship in the West until the Carolingian period around 800 CE. Even then the efforts of the Carolingians to import the Christian message into the west failed when the Carolingian empire disintegrated in the generation after Charlemagne. Christianity was not to be revived again until the battles between the popes and the emperors over the investiture issue in the 1200s. But once again the balance of forces in the West tipped against reception of the Christian message when the scholastic philosophers produced an interpretation of the monarchy that favored the primacy of the popes over the emperors or kings. The last chance for Christianity in Europe occurred at the time of the Reformation when both the popes and the Protestant reformers attempted to rein in abuses of the priesthood but failed. The Protestants simply eliminated the priests by eliminating the basic sacrificial rites of the Church, while the Catholics were never able to formulate a theology of the sacred kingship despite contributions from émigré Byzantine theologians (like Bessarion) until the twentieth century when Pope Pius XI published the encyclical *Quas Primas* in 1925. By that time, however, the monarchies of Europe had gone through a phase of despotism, which then issued in revolts and the death of monarchy itself in Europe. All that, as they say, is now history. During those dark times when Europe operated without a sacred kingship and then a despotic caricature of the divine kingship during the premodern, post-Renaissance era, demonic possession phenomena became ubiquitous. In what remains of this chapter we trace the themes of demonic possession in the canonical scriptures of the New Testament. From its origins in early Christianity we will then in subsequent chapters trace its history in Europe up to the modern age.

EXORCISMS IN THE GOSPEL OF MATTHEW

The New Testament mentions several occasions when Jesus or one of the apostles performed an exorcism. I will focus here only on the Gospel of Matthew.

In Matt. 4:23–25 we hear that among all the cures and healings that Jesus performed in the Galilee were also the curing of demon-possessed persons. In Matt. 8:16–17 Jesus drove out demons with a "word" and then there is a reference to the divine kingship as follows:

> [6]When evening came, many who were demon-possessed were brought to him, and he drove out the spirits with a word and healed all the sick. This was to fulfill what was spoken through the prophet Isaiah: "He took up our infirmities and carried our diseases."

Now of course, as we have seen in volume 1, traditionally it was the divine king in his capacity as the scapegoat who was slated and destined to carry the impurities and infirmities of the kingdom so that they could be eliminated sacrificially by the killing of the king or a substitute. We know that the New Testament authors specifically saw Jesus as a divine king who became the scapegoat for the sins of all of humanity. Thus, it is fascinating to see this reference to the role of the divine kingship right when Jesus performed an exorcism. The fact that Jesus used "a word" (presumably a command) to cast out the demon suggests that Jesus spoke with the authority of both the king and the priest (like Melchizedek) and that Jesus possessed secret knowledge of healing rituals derived from initiation into specialized religious societies (perhaps like the Essenes or the cult around John the Baptist) that proliferated in the intertestamental period in Palestine.

In Matt. 8:28-34: Jesus sent a herd of demons from two men into a herd of about *two thousand* pigs (in Mark 5:1–20; and Luke 8:26–39, however, there is only one man possessed by many demons called Legion).

> [8]When he arrived at the other side in the region of the Gadarenes, two demon-possessed men coming from the tombs met him. They were so violent that no one could pass that way. "What do you want with us, Son of God?" they shouted. "Have you come here to torture us before the appointed time?" Some distance from them a large herd of pigs was feeding. The demons begged Jesus, "If you drive us out, send us into the herd of pigs." He said to them, "Go!" So they came out and went into the pigs, and the whole herd rushed down the steep bank into the lake and died in the water. Those tending the pigs ran off, went into the town and reported all this, including what had happened to the demon-possessed men. Then the whole town went out to meet Jesus. And when they saw him, they pleaded with him to leave their region.

I have written about this episode in volume 1 so will only briefly comment on it here. The great theologian Rudolf Bultmann suggested that this episode exemplified all of the other exorcism "miracle healings" in the New Testament scriptures. First there is a meeting or mutual recognition between Jesus and the demons. Then we get a description of the affliction caused by the demons. Then the demons attempt to evade the exorcism. This fails and Jesus performs the exorcism with a command or some other gesture of authority. The demons are expelled, the person appears cured, and spectators are awed.

Note that this same basic sequence of ritual gestures occurs in ritual healings associated with the divine kings in a multitude of cultures across a multitude of historical periods—even in Western Europe. A sick individual was brought before the king during a special ritual service. Normally no one was allowed to touch the king on pain of death. Thus the king's royal touch was special and sacred. Once the individual was presented to the king the affliction was displayed or uncovered or verbally represented to the king. The king would then verbally pronounce a word or command that abjured the illness or commanded the illness to leave the patient. This abjuration is done with all the pomp of authority and office. Then the royal touch occurred. Often this was a laying on of hands. A courtier would then pronounce the illness defeated. Spectators would then be awed and so on.

Jesus' method of exorcism, as exemplified in the episode of the Gerasene demoniac, essentially involves the assertion of royal authority. Jesus has authority over all other powers and principalities including the worlds of demons. This royal authority is then passed onto the apostles and the Church (e.g., see Matt. 10:1–8). The exorcism ritual of the church retains this essential element of command and authority down to the present day.

In Matt. 9:32–33: we see this ritual sequence of events, truncated somewhat, but essentially intact when Jesus cured a mute:

> As they went out, behold, they brought to him a dumb man possessed with a devil. And when the devil was cast out, the dumb spake: and the multitudes marvelled, saying, It was never so seen in Israel.

In Matt. 12:22–32, Jesus healed a demon-possessed blind and dumb man and the people took this as evidence of Jesus' divine kingship:

> Then they brought him a demon-possessed man who was blind and mute, and Jesus healed him, so that he could both talk and see. All the people were astonished and said, "Could this be the Son of David?"

In Matt. 15:21–28, Jesus is shown to act when the afflicted express faith in him as a divine king:

[21] Leaving that place, Jesus withdrew to the region of Tyre and Sidon. A Canaanite woman from that vicinity came to him, crying out, "Lord, Son of David, have mercy on me! My daughter is suffering terribly from demon-possession." Jesus did not answer a word. So his disciples came to him and urged him, "Send her away, for she keeps crying out after us." He answered, "I was sent only to the lost sheep of Israel." The woman came and knelt before him. "Lord, help me!" she said. He replied, "It is not right to take the children's bread and toss it to their dogs." "Yes, Lord," she said, "but even the dogs eat the crumbs that fall from their masters' table." Then Jesus answered, "Woman, you have great faith! Your request is granted." And her daughter was healed from that very hour.

Note that this episode makes modern readers, ideologically indoctrinated with the virtues of tolerance and respect for other cultures, cringe. Jesus seems to speak like an arrogant bigot to this poor woman whose daughter is suffering from a terrible affliction. But certain details in the story suggest that Jesus is observing the rules of healing by the sacred kingship. He is King of the Jews, not the Canaanites. Healings for the Canaanites should therefore not be possible unless they became his subjects. This woman voluntarily submits to Jesus, calling him Lord (or King) and kneeling before him as a vassal or subject would do before a king. Not even the Canaanites would kneel before a mere miracle worker or prophet. Only a king would elicit that kind of reverence or "faith." By her act of submission she makes herself the subject of Jesus. Jesus therefore draws the logical conclusion and issues the appropriate authoritative word.

These few examples of Jesus' exorcisms suffices, it seems to me, to give us a picture of how Jesus created the template from which the Western tradition would draw its procedures for ritual exorcism in the centuries to come. We have seen that Jesus either consciously or unconsciously drew on the tradition of healings by the sacred kings of the ancient Near East. The key event in each exorcism is the voice of authority—royal authority that commands the demon to depart. Jesus thus revived and built upon the tradition of royal healings—of the divine kingship to perform his ministries. In volume 1 I showed how the New Testament authors claimed that the divine kingship of Christ was a central message of Christianity. This message was preserved in Eastern forms of Christianity but was never consolidated in either the East or the West. We will see that the West produced spectacular episodes and cases of demonic possession because it lacked a tradition of a sacred kingship. The popes and the priests were therefore politically strong. The religious theology of Christianity emphasized the cosmic battle between good and evil in a way that rivaled the corresponding apocalyptical theologies of Zoroastrianism and intertestamental Judaism. The source of these potent theologies of a warfare between good and evil was, of course, the holy scriptures of the New Testament canon. With these elements of a weak kingship—a potent priesthood and an explicit theology of a cosmic battle between good and evil with a full description or demonology of the evil forces—it seems almost inevitable that demonic possession phenomena would emerge as important events in the history of the West.

Chapter 9

Devils, Witches, and the Birth of Modernity in Europe

In previous chapters of this volume and its companion volume, we have traced the history of both negative and positive forms of spirit possession. We have seen that positive forms of spirit possession are generally self-regulated or controlled by the individual. They are voluntary in the sense that the possession experience can be started and ended by the individual himself. The spirit that informed the consciousness of the possessed individual in cases of positive possession is generally holy, moral, and well disposed toward others. Its ethic is self-sacrificial and one of service to others. It speaks with authority and command and it enriches the individual in the sense that it frees the individual from responding to attention-grabbing stimuli in the present moment and allows for planning for future contingencies.

Involuntary possession, on the other hand, whether it is demonic or nondemonic, does not tend to enrich the individual but rather tends toward destructive social consequences. It tends to involve deindividuation and a shifting of the identity of the individual over to the group. The individual lives for the group instead of for "the self in relation to the god." Mass or group hysteria is often associated with demonic forms of possession. There is a loss of individual autonomy and an enhancement of group energy, group strength, and group hysteria. Ultimately the group hysteria leads to mania and calls for blood. There is a mockery of things set apart as holy and an enhancement of idiocy and violence toward things or persons set apart as sacred. In demonic possession frenzy is valued as a thing in itself because it invariably leads to the shedding of blood and the violent killing of an innocent. The frenzied tearing to pieces of defenseless persons or peoples is the mark of the demonic. Manic, violent, restlessness is the normal ontologic state of the group. The individual, the true autonomous, authoritative individual is the enemy of the group. He is the annihilation and cancellation of the group—this restless fury, this frenzied self-destructiveness. The individual, therefore, must be destroyed at all costs or prevented from being manifested at all costs.

Historically, demonic attacks on the phenomena of the individual had to start with demonic attacks on the sacred kingship, as the roots of the individual are in the sacred kingship. The king, for centuries, exemplified the ethic of holy spirit possession and the dignity and authority of the autonomous individual. In the beginning, the kingly archetype as we understand it today was carried by the shamans of the Upper Paleolithic and then the early chiefdoms and kingships of the Neolithic. The kings came into their own in the traditional societies of the first civilizations that arose in Egypt and the Near East and elsewhere. These civilizations were born out of ritual centers like the great megalithic monumental sites in Western Europe and the festival/sacrificial sites like Gobele Teke in Turkey. The first civilizations saw the birth of both the sacred kingship and the individual consciousness and conscience. We see the individual consciousness reflected in the wisdom literature of the ancient Near East, for example. This trend towards the exaltation of the individual dignity, despite the suffering associated with individuality came to full realization in the cultures and religions of the axial age (initiated by Zoroaster). These religions and cultures all testified to the fact that the individual must choose between good and evil. The individual was free to choose a course of action that may or may not lead to tragedy but would in the final analysis lead to a kind of redemption. But just when this trend in individuation peaked in the birth of the axial age religions, the sacred kingship came under concerted attack from two directions: the universalizing empires/emperors in various parts of the world and the proliferation of fertility cults all around the world. All around the world the strongest of the kings sought to end war and to enrich themselves by conquering the entire world and creating one vast, unified empire. To do so the emperors had to clarify the role of local kingships. Were they as sacred as the emperor? If not, why not? And what was the obligation of the local man to the local king and the universal emperor? Thus the local sacred kingships were devalued when they lost their power and charisma under the emperors.

While the world conquering emperors of Egypt, China, the Eurasian steppes, and the Mideast (Alexander, Cyrus, and the Romans) sought to unify the world under one rule, periodic outbreaks of mass hysteria in the form of fertility cults undermined the social order instilled by the sacred kingship more generally. These fertility cults, while present during the period of the Upper Paleolithic, became much more prevalent and prominent during the period of the Neolithic when the sacred kingship first took form. Goddess and mother worship became a very powerful and ubiquitous form of religious practice. The culture of Minoan Crete, the temples at Malta, the Venus figurines, and the rock art from various Neolithic European sites all testify to the power of these fertility cults to control people's lives, particularly women's lives. Opposed to these far flung and female-predominant fertility cults were the secret male societies. These were the societies, according to some, that created the great cave art sites of the Upper Paleolithic. They also gave birth to the sacred kingship and they built the great ritual centers that gave birth to the first urban centers in the Near East. From the beginning these male cults operated independent of and opposed to the female cults and vice versa. The female cults did not allow males to view their rituals and the male cults did not allow females to view their rituals. To do so meant death for the spy. The rituals were sacred. The spy could pollute whole societies by violating the sacred mysteries of sexual life. Although the male cults "opposed" the female cults and vice versa, they did so for ritual reasons—not for purposes of misogyny or political supremacy. It was understood that if a man violated the secrecy of the female rituals it was acceptable for the women to tear that man to pieces. Conversely, if a woman mocked or transgressed any of the male cult rituals she could be put to death by the men.

When in the ritual state if a man touched or was touched by a menstruating women he was considered unclean. Women supported this conception of the uncleanness of menstruation as it gave them protection against marauding men who raped and pillaged their way through village after village. Conversely, if a women spied on one of the secret male rituals (e.g., carving a fetish or a mask) the woman was considered to have committed a transgression and thus was unclean. Again the women supported this practice as it kept the spheres of women and men separate and gave women protection and some modicum of power derived from their group activities. The men's secret societies also tended to turn boys into men via initiation rites. These men would learn to fight, to hunt and to be fathers—all skills women necessarily needed in their men. Women therefore supported the male societies and men supported the female societies. It was understood that they were necessary for the continuation of the cosmos.

Despite the support of one another's secret rituals there were tensions between the sexes that led to conflict as well. The secret male societies emphasized initiatory ordeals and the production of a kingly authoritative character. The fertility cults, on the other hand, emphasized immersion in a group ecstasy, the sacrifice of self for children and others, and the exaltation of sex and the sacredness of sex. Women depended on others for help in raising children while men could function essentially as lone hunters. Women therefore gravitated toward the group for expression and protection and men did not. Women were more social and men were more antisocial. This fundamental antagonism between the sexes is a reality of life and cannot be written off as a kind of vestigial organ of biology of no consequence. This sex difference in the roles of reproduction infused and informed all of humanity's ritual and religious practices. Religious practices in turn created the political orders we are all heir to. Nevertheless, a war of the sexes is not inevitable or even necessary.

Humanity has produced a solution to this war in the form of the sacred kingship. The sacred kingship involved both authoritative rule and self-sacrificial service to the community. The kingship became the model for men. The king created order out of political chaos and protected the weak and the poor against the violent. The king, via his special role as the carrier of the community values and spirit, and because of the fact that he was the only person who had a formal relationship with all other members of the community, he necessarily cumulated the impurities of all these individuals. The impurities, all of them, could be eliminated through sacrificing the king and this is what was done for millennia. As the kingship became more politically vital for the machinery of government it became more expensive to kill an experienced king and thus substitute sacrificial rites were invented. Their function was the same—to eliminate impurities in the community. The king performed these sacrifices but then delegated these powers to the priests. The kingship, even with the addition of the priesthood, was an effective solution when it first appeared in the Neolithic and it remains a viable one to this day. To see why take a look at the period of European history between the late 1400s and the late 1600s—between the Renaissance and the Enlightenment—the period that created the witch hunts, the absolutist monarchies, and modernity itself.

In this period of "early modern Europe" people had rediscovered the ancients. Hermetic lore, Kabbala, astrology, alchemy, and the embryonic forms of the sciences were all in full swing. Thus, Newton, one of the greatest scientists of all time, could be an obsessed alchemist and mystic at the same time. Newton's codiscoverer of the calculus, the great philosopher Leibnitz, simultaneously espoused the power of reason and the power of the magical arts. He very likely was a member of the secret male society— the Rosicrucians. Men like Leibnitz, Spinoza, Descartes, and others were formulating a complete and logically coherent philosophy of the dignity of the individual against the claims of the group. Leibnitz's monadology, in particular, was a major contribution on the theory of uniqueness and individuality.

Despite all these interesting developments the period was character-ized by a lack of any clearly visible form of the sacred kingship. The Byz-antine empire had just been overthrown by the Ottomans in the previous century. The Holy Roman emperor was merely a titular figure who could not effectively rule any of the princes who supposedly owed him hom-age. Germany was a patchwork of a huge range of petty principalities and powers. With the advent of Luther in the early 1500s and the rise of the Protestant Reformation in the mid-1500s Europe itself was divided along confessional lines and the wars of religion soon took center stage, eclips-ing the power of any monarchy that attempted to ride the religious tiger into rule. The whole continent was thrown into war by the fanaticism of the Protestant Reformation and the violence of the Catholic attempt to reverse Protestant gains. There simply was no strong sacred kingship in Europe during this period. Nevertheless the social forces unleashed dur-ing this period gave rise to the absolutist monarchies of Europe that ended up ruling Europe into the modern era. These monarchies, in turn, gave rise to the modern state as we know it today and thus of modernity itself.

Why did the absolutist monarchies emerge in Europe at this time? One factor was the rise of millennial heresies and ecstatic cults throughout Europe during these centuries. The old complex of the sacred kingship operated to keep these types of destructive popular cults in check. With-out the kingship the cults proliferated. If the sacrificial rites were seen as ineffective (due to the absence of the kingship or a corrupt or absent priesthood) the people had to find a way to eliminate impurities in the society and their ways were always violent and tragic. There were also all kinds of natural catastrophes like the black death and climatic crises that periodically blighted the continent during this period. War, constant war, was another factor but finally the major factor that gave rise to absolutist forms of monarchy in this period was the religious situation: (1) there was no sacred kingship, (2) the priesthood was in decline due to the Protes-tant Reformation, and (3) popular forms of religiosity filled the vacuum and these tended to be ecstatic cults and millenialist in flavor. These latter social forces tend to social disorder because they depend on group fervor and irrational group dynamics to stay alive.

Governments have always and everywhere acted to oppose these sorts of ecstatic cults precisely because they are inimical to social order and sta-bility. But the clash between government and cult inevitably leads to blood-shed and the resultant "growth under persecution" of the cultist groups. In response the governments themselves must grow or die and thus there is an arms race between cult and government until one or the other loses. In premodern Europe the governments became centralized and strong and they crushed all kinds of popular phenomena along the way—among them the ecstatic cults. Another social group that got in the way of the government machine was the mass hysterical phenomena known as the witch's craze. In response to the accusations of witchcraft that seemed to spout like weeds all over Europe and North America in those days governments everywhere began witch hunts and the infamous witch trials. By the time the witch mania had been stamped out, up between 50,000 and 100,000 people had been executed for witchcraft.

Interestingly enough, just as in the ancient Neolithic period, the ecstatic cults that are indexed by the witch trials and witch-hunts in premodern Europe involved predominantly female groups accused of or practicing fertility rituals of one kind or another along with frenzied group effects and then an overwhelmingly brutal government response. Young women and children were virtually always the accusers. They became frenzied, claiming attack by a witch, and then they demanded blood. For example, teenage girls might accuse the local old maid of harming them with witchcraft or the local priest of bewitching them. Mass hysteria ensues. The public is alarmed. Some local authority figure uses these accusations to prosecute the accused. The accused are then tortured and executed. When the accusers are adults, they too are often tortured and executed as well. In short, blood is shed in response to the demand. Next, the women who demand the blood are themselves punished, often with a ferocity that staggers the imagination. The old Neolithic pattern of ecstatic female cults demanding sacrificial blood and getting it, in spades, from the government, is seen here to still operate in premodern Europe.

The *Malleus Maleficarum*, by Kramer and Sprenger, was published in 1487/1971, signaling the rise of the witch mania. It became a kind of handbook for witch hunters during the height of the witch craze in the following century. I will survey only a handful of cases of witch scares and trials—choosing those that might carry lessons for a general theory of spirit possession and of cultural modernity.

NORTH BERWICK WITCH TRIALS IN SCOTLAND (1590)

The North Berwick witch trials were interesting because they helped define the kingship of premodern Scotland and England. King James VI of Scotland (later King James I of England) participated in the trials. The trials took place in the St. Andrew's Auld Kirk in North Berwick. They ran for two years and implicated 70 people. The confessions were extracted by torture. King James VI had been convinced that witches had stirred up storms to prevent his marriage to Princess Anne, sister of Christian IV, king of Denmark. She could not cross the channel due to storms so he repeatedly tried to go to her but was stymied by storms himself. When he finally retrieved her, storms threatened their safety on the return trip. Once back in Scotland there were repeated attempts on his life, some of which he thought were plotted by witches. He became convinced that some of the accused were guilty when one of the witches told him of a private conversation he had had with Anne on the return journey. Many of the accused were brutally tortured—some in front of James himself.

James later wrote a book, the *Daemonologie* (1597/1969), in which he defended the reality of demonic spirits and the dangerousness of witchcraft. Interestingly he defined a witch as "a consulter of familiar spirits." A *familiar spirit* is a spirit being who is: (1) conjured by ritual magic, (2) controlled by the conjurer via ritual magic, (3) made to serve the wishes of the conjurer, and (4) is typically housed in some fetish object. Familiars were believed to be low-level demons given by Satan to a witch after she signed a pact in blood with Satan. Witches tended to keep their familiars in living animals like black cats rather than in bottles or fetish objects. When James became king of England he ensured strengthening of legislation against witches. The original witchcraft act of 1604 made it a crime to "consult, covenant with, entertain, employ, feed, or reward any evil and wicked spirit to or for any intent or purpose." James saw to it that these laws were enforced. James later restrained the laws that enjoined brutal torture but throughout his life he believed in the reality and danger of witchcraft. James also was interested in the theory and theology of the sacred kingship. Thus he combines in his own person our two themes of the sacred kingship and destructive ecstatic cults.

James wrote two works: *The True Law of Free Monarchies* (1598/1930) and *Daemonologie* (1597/1969). While *The True Law of Free Monarchies* work is often considered nothing but a tract to justify an absolutist version of monarchical rule, James actually was at pains to argue that the kingship entailed service to the realm and obedience under God. He defended the kingship as essentially a religious institution not subject to papal or parliamentary deposition but of course subject to right reason, the natural law, and tradition. The king embodies the godhead and his person is sacred but for these very reasons he must live a life of sacrifice for his people. James understood that the primary religious and legal institution of any and every civilization is the kingship. Before laws were made or parliaments convened or before social classes were formed there existed the leader or king that formed the community in the first place. The king is therefore the foundation of social order and must be considered sacred. His powers are constrained by tradition and by God, that is, Christian prudence and moral law. Despite this apparently sophisticated if not perfect understanding of the sacred kingship James was not a perfect or ideal king. Nevertheless, he was an adequate king and he gave Britain some desperately needed stability for a brief period of time . . . but it was to be merely a brief respite before the storm. His work was squandered by his son Charles. The fanatical Puritans ended the sacred kingship once and for all in Europe when they executed Charles.

Meanwhile, just as happened with James in Scotland, in France a developing monarchy was defining itself against popular manias. Once again those manias took the form of witch crazes and witch trials.

AIX-EN-PROVENCE POSSESSIONS (1609–1611)

In 1605 a 12-year-old girl from an aristocratic Provencal (the region centuries earlier of the Cathar heresy and related wars) family was sent to an Ursuline convent in Aix-en-Provence. The convent housed six other nuns, all from wealthy or aristocratic backgrounds and presumably sent to the convent because they either could not be married off or they wished not to be married but instead had a genuine religious vocation. The 12-year-old girl took the religious name of Sister Madeleine de Demandolx de la Palud. After about two years of religious life she became severely depressed and was sent home. The family enlisted the help of a priest father, Louis Gaufridi, a handsome personable man who sought to help the young girl. Unfortunately for Father Gaufridi, Sister Madeleine fell violently in love with him. In 1607 she was sent back to the convent and roughly two years later she began evidencing signs of demonic possession. She had fits, smashed crucifixes, and saw demons. Her manic fits began to infect the other nuns and soon several were experiencing convulsions and seeing demons. Sister Madeleine then accused Father Gaufridi of seducing her, of denying God, and of having commerce with demons. She claimed that the priest had given her a drink to cause an abortion in case she became pregnant. The confessor for the nuns at the convent began a series of exorcisms on Madeleine. But they failed to work.

Meanwhile the other nuns' possession displays became quite dramatic as well. The confessor took them to be exorcised by the regional inquisitor who had executed witches in the past but this exorcism failed as well. The nuns by this time had become manic and hysterical, putting on dramatic performances of demonic signs such as speaking in low male voices, of bodily contortions, mouthing obscenities, and so on. On the strength of the accusations of the hysterical nuns, Gaufridi was arrested as a sorcerer. Sister Madeleine by this time appeared psychotic, dancing like a wild woman, neighing like a horse, and claiming attendance at nighttime sabbats where babies were sacrificed and eaten by participants. Twice she attempted suicide. Gaufridi was convicted of sorcery on the testimony of the hysterical nuns. He was horribly tortured after being kept in chains for months in a rat-infested dungeon. He was strung up on a rope and then dropped to break his bones. He was hoisted on a rope with weights on his feet and then dropped to dislocate and break his bones. He was dragged through the streets of Aix for five hours. He was scheduled to be burned alive but the bishop granted him a dispensation to be strangled before being burned. He was then strangled and burned. But the hysterical nuns were not finished with the killing of innocents. One of them a few years later claimed that a blind girl was a witch and the poor unfortunate was then burned at the stake in 1611. The mania then spread to young girls in the villages and people began to see witches everywhere. Old women and young men were the major targets of the young girls' hysterical accusations.

THE LOUDUN POSSESSIONS (1630–1634)

The witch manias in 1600s France peaked with the so-called Loudun possessions in 1630. Once again the case involved hysterical nuns accusing a handsome priest of bewitchment and that priest being brutally tortured and murdered on the testimony of these crazed and bloodthirsty young girls.

In 1617 Father Urbain Grandier was appointed parish priest of St-Pierre-du-Marche in Loudun, a town in Poitiers, France. Grandier was handsome, well educated, and politically well connected. He was also intelligent, writing a learned treatise against the celibacy of priests. He was also arrogant and indiscreet. He soon became involved with Philippa Trincant, the daughter of the king's solicitor in Loudun and may have fathered her child. In addition to Trincant, Grandier also acquired Madeleine de Brou, daughter of the king's councillor in Loudun as a mistress.

Meanwhile the Mother Superior of a nearby Ursuline convent, Sister Jeanne des Anges, invited Grandier to become father confessor to the nuns at the convent but Grandier declined. Sometime later Sister Jeanne began to evidence signs of possession. She had convulsions and began speaking in tongues. Soon many of the other nuns at the convent began having dreams and nightmares. Sister Jeanne confessed to the father director of the convent, a Father Mignon, that she had been bewitched by Grandier. Then many of the other nuns began to make similar claims.

Fathers Mignon and his aide, Father Barre, concluded that the nuns were possessed by demons and immediately proceeded to perform exorcisms on the possessed nuns. Several of the nuns, including Sister Jeanne, suffered violent convulsions during the procedure. They would suddenly bark, scream, blaspheme, and contort their bodies. During the exorcisms, Jeanne swore that she and the other nuns were possessed by two demons named Asmodeus and Zabulon. These demons were sent to the nuns when Father Grandier tossed a bouquet of roses over the convent walls.

Grandier realized that he was about to be arrested for sorcery on the testimony of the hysterical nuns and so he appealed to the archbishop of Bordeaux. The archbishop cleared Grandier of the charges and ordered the nuns to cease the hysterics.

Unfortunately for Grandier one of the nuns in the convent was a relative of the powerful Cardinal Richelieu. Grandier unwisely had opposed Richelieu on a couple of occasions so Richelieu had no love for Grandier. Richelieu is an important historical character in the story of the decline of the sacred kingship and the rise of the absolutist monarchies in Europe. His power was second only to the king and was the king's first councilor. He was generally considered to be the man behind the centralization of state powers into the hands of the king in France. Richelieu essentially created the conditions in France for the glorious reign of the Sun King a few decades hence. Richelieu himself seemed not to have considered the king a religious office per se but he also did not think it wise or just that the king should be subordinate to the papacy. In any case Richelieu's intervention into the Loudun affair all but assured the destruction of Grandier at the hands of the hysterical nuns. Richelieu overruled the archbishop and ordered a commission to look into the Grandier affair and staffed it with Grandier's enemies.

When exorcisms resumed at Loudun, they now became a political and public spectacle. Amazingly up to 7,000 spectators attended these lurid shows. By now Sister Jeanne and her nuns claimed to be possessed by Isacarron, the devil of debauchery. The exorcisms in turn became spectacles with the hysterical nuns going through all kinds of sexual pantomimes and bodily contortions. A devil's pact allegedly written between the devil and Grandier was produced. This note was written in Jeanne's hand.

When the trial commenced it was all but certain that Grandier would be convicted of sorcery, tortured and executed. This is in fact what happened. Grandier's legs were broken. He was tortured on the rack, his bones were broken with sledgehammers. He was partially hanged and then burned alive—all because of the deranged nuns' accusations.

THE SALEM WITCH TRIALS (1692–1693)

Some 60 years after the Loudun outrages, a similar set of outrages would occur halfway across the world and in a totally different culture—the Puritan culture of the New World in Salem, Massachusetts. Once again a handful of young girls began to claim bewitchment. This time the targets were both men and older women. Once again these innocents were convicted on the hysterical testimonies of deranged girls. Once again the executions would be brutal and senseless. Once again the same forces were at play: a frenzied group of young woman calling for blood and a government all too willing to provide them with it. Once again there was mania among young girls, sexual intrigue, accusations of witchery against spotless men and defenseless women, powerful politicians who use the spectacle for political purposes and brutal executions.

On the strength of the accusations of the hysterical girls over 150 people were arrested and imprisoned. Dozens were executed by hanging. At least five more of the accused died in prison.

In his book *Memorable Providences Relating to Witchcrafts and Possessions* (1689), Cotton Mather had described possession in four children of Boston who were supposedly bewitched by an Irish washerwoman, Mary Glover. Mather later became an adviser to the magistrates trying the cases of the accused in Salem.

In Salem in 1692, Betty Parris, age 9, and her cousin Abigail Williams, age 11, the daughter and niece (respectively) of the Reverend Samuel Parris, began to have fits, and to utter strange sounds, while contorting themselves into peculiar bodily postures. These manic behaviors started to spread to other young women in the village. They too began to yell and scream during church services and to go into weird bodily contortions. They claimed that they had been bewitched by Sarah Good, an indigent old woman, Sarah Osborne (a woman of ill repute), and Tituba, a slave of Native American background who occasionally played with the girls. These three defenseless women were jailed for later trial. Meanwhile the hysterical girls began to accuse others of being witches as well. This time they targeted older women of impeccable reputations. All were, nevertheless jailed and put on trial. When a Mr. John Proctor protested the trials he too was arrested. Further accusations by the hysterical girls ensued eventually implicating dozens of people as witches. The girls claimed they knew these people were witches because their specters haunted them. Even though the use of spectral evidence was considered problematic given the obvious ways in which the girls could fake this "evidence," spectral evidence was nevertheless used to indict, convict, and hang innocent men and women. Such is the power of the mania that seizes a group when mass hysteria spreads. All rational thinking ceases and hysterical girls are put in charge of the polity. They, however, want one thing: blood. The government usually gives it to them if no sacred kingship is present to call a halt to the madness. No sacred kingship was present in the colonies—the English had just a generation previously killed their king. The subsequent kings were weak and uninspiring. Meanwhile, Sarah Osborne, one of the first three accused, died in jail on May 10, 1692.

Eventually 62 people were put on trial for witchcraft in Salem. A grand jury of ostensibly intelligent and just citizens tended to endorse all the accusations the children made against the defendants no matter how outlandish. As in the Scottish and the French cases, court examiners offered the most ludicrous evidence in support of charges of witchery such as devil's marks (or blemishes) on the body that were insensitive to touch. The so-called touch-test involved the accused being required to touch or lay hands on their accusers to see what effect it had. If the girls went into fits then that meant that the accused were indeed witches. It is difficult to understand how the magistrates could accept such evidence.

The first conviction and hanging occurred by June 1692. Another elderly person died in jail in June as well. Five people were executed on July 19, 1692. Another six were executed in August. Before being executed, George Burroughs recited the Lord's Prayer perfectly, something that was impossible for a demonically possessed person, but Cotton Mather urged execution anyway. Yet more executions by hanging followed. In September Giles Corey was pressed beneath an increasingly heavy load of stones, in an attempt to make him confess to sorcery. He was 80 years old and died under the weight of stones. Another eight people were convicted and hanged in July–August of that year.

In January 1693 the manic killing of the accused showed every sign of continuing. More people were found guilty and sentenced to death but the governor finally intervened and put an end to the farcical trials.

SUMMARY OF WITCH CRAZE PHENOMENA

I could provide multiple examples of further manias and witch crazes from this period of history. It is interesting that just a couple of centuries before the onset of the witch crazes and immediately after the peak of the manic killings in the 1690s governments and intellectuals everywhere decried accusations of witchery as superstitious nonsense and the ravings of hysterical girls. The great rationalist scholastic philosophers of the Middle Ages railed against the idiocies of these sorts of accusations. Even back as far as Charlemagne (around 800 CE) accusations of witchery by hysterical girls were considered with profound suspicion. Similarly right after the witch craze ended people and governments everywhere decried the abuses of the witch trials. So the madness lasted only from the late 1400s to the late 1600s. It is important to point out that though the young girls were most often the foci of the wave of madness that would seep through whole communities, these communities nevertheless were infected by popular and mass hysteria as well. Crowds reveled in the spectacle of possessions and neighbors accused neighbors of witchcraft and devil worship. Groups of people became lynch mobs and painted lurid portraits in their minds of witches' Sabbaths and bloody infant sacrifices. The waves of madness would grip whole communities and prevent even the best citizens from thinking clearly. Instead the manias of the young girls would initiate a wave of hysteria, shutting down minds, closing off compassion for the accused, and heightening the calls for blood. What sort of social process could cause this kind of blood lust and mob mentality?

It is not enough to say that powerful institutions like the local and federal governments took advantage of the madness to build their own power. The government could not do that without some emotional support from the local people. What happened to these people? What induced them to take the accusations of witchcraft seriously? It must have been something powerful, atavistic, primitive, and compelling. My own feeling is that these people sensed that the normal mechanisms for purging impurities from this system had broken down and thus their minds became attuned to identification of potential scapegoats that could carry the sins of the community so that those sins could be destroyed in the person of the scapegoat. Why is it that hysteria of young girls triggers this subconscious need for purification? It must be that the young girls subconsciously recall those primitive taboos around male and female secret rites. In primitive societies, young girls who had had their first menstruation would be placed into groups of other young females all dancing to a fertility goddess. They danced till they became frenzied and possessed by the goddess. Then sacrificial rites were performed. Men were not allowed to see these rites on pain of death. These sacrificial rites invariably ended in the tearing to pieces of a sacrificial animal and the smearing of the victim's blood onto participants in the rites. Frenzied ecstatic possession rites were a constant of all premodern societies. It was understood that these rites were inherently destructive and had to be controlled and opposed by the sacred kingship in traditional societies.

But why were the female ecstatic cults and witches considered evil? Yes, they tended to create social disorder when they formed groups, but there were many other ecstatic cults that created social disorder and they weren't necessarily branded as satanic or demonic. Witches were. Why? Again I connect this to the absence of any strong sacred kingship in Europe. A major function of the sacred kingship is that it eliminates impurities from the community through the sacrifice either of the king himself or of some suitable substitute. When the community has no sacred kingship or when the king and his priesthood are seen as ineffective, then the sacrificial rites are seen as ineffective as well. When that happens all kinds of people begin to accumulate impurities and those most vulnerable (e.g., old maids who act in eccentric ways) are made the scapegoat in the strict sense of that religious term. They are made into sacred receptacles that are filled up with sin and impurity and then killed or eliminated from the community in order to cleanse the community of impurity. Many scholars of the witch hunts of premodern Europe have pointed to the scapegoat features of the trial and execution of women accused of witchery. I add here only a hypothesis that the scapegoat mechanism was operative due to the lack of any visible sacred kingship on the European scene. Up to the 1500s both the Byzantine and the Holy Roman emperors had provided some semblance of the sacred kingship for Europeans but by the end of the 1500s both institutions had either vanished or were in political deadlock. Politics abhors a power vacuum. Into that vacuum rushed the ecstatic groups and cults that then filtered down to influence the popular imagination.

Chapter 10

The Roman Ritual
of Exorcism

We have taken the story of demonic possession in the West up to the modern era. I now want to look at the ritual of exorcism that is most often used for exorcisms in the West in the modern era. This is the Roman Catholic rite of exorcism. For those Christian congregations still professing some belief in the reality of the demonic realm, many offer procedures for protection from demons or exorcism or expulsion of demons. At a minimum, prayer and fasting is used to expel demons from the minds of the possessed. More often, prayer and fasting are supplemented with the laying on of hands and verbal commands to the demon to leave the soul of the possessed. Relative to the ancient rite of exorcism that developed in the West and to the rites for exorcism used in the Eastern Orthodox, confessions of these procedures seem bereft, threadbare, and impoverished. They are, nevertheless, very similar to the procedures used by the earliest Christian communities. To that extent, they are truer to the earliest Christian witness than the rite that developed in the West and used in the West up to the modern era.

On the other hand, the rite used in the West incorporates prayer, fasting, commands, and laying on of hands as well. Thus, the rite has what the earliest Christian communities used to cast out demons and, in addition, has other means as well. In my view, the rites developed by the Medieval and post-Reformation (and the Byzantine/Eastern rite) churches are superior to those of the early Christians. Although Jesus used rituals and techniques that were similar to what the early Christians used to cast out demons, he was a king and he spoke with authority. He explicitly said that the exorcisms were proof of his royal status and messiahship. These rituals were, therefore, effective in his hands. Jesus himself had given the apostles authority to cast out demons, but it took centuries for the Church to learn to use that authority effectively.

The modern rite of exorcism in the Roman Catholic Church preserves the ancient Christian practices and adds to them additional prayers and practices. It is the rite that the West has used for centuries to battle the demonic and it has influenced spirit-possession phenomena in the West for centuries. I will argue that its psychologic and spiritual efficacy comes from its ability to mimic royal sacrificial rites that go back to the Neolithic sacrifices of the king.

Exorcism is essentially a modern echo of the ancient royal blood sacrifice with the possessed person acting as the scapegoat who is loaded with impurities of the community. Like the kings of primeval memory, the possessed individual is supernaturalized before the sacrificial rite can be performed. The demon represents the supernaturalized victim that will be expelled or sacrificed. Jesus' spirit-possession experiences followed the pattern of royal initiation and sacrifice. Jesus himself explicitly says that like the kings of old he must offer himself as a sacrifice for the people. The king had to be physically and spiritually without blemish so that he could accumulate the impurities of a community into his person. He had to shoulder the sins of the people so that those sins could be expelled or destroyed. They were destroyed by destroying or sacrificing the person who carried them for the people. In his capacity as a spotless and blameless victim or scapegoat, the king becomes spiritualized or supernaturalized. When they put to death the king, they also put to death a god. Jesus, too, understood his sacrifice in similar terms. He took on himself all the sins of the world and then he was killed and the sins of the world were destroyed as well.

Such is the mythological understanding of the king's sacrifice. Now what happens when this sacrificial mechanism is not working in a society? In that case, vulnerable people step forward and offer themselves as candidates to take on the sins and impurities of the community. But, given the fact that they are not kings, it is much more difficult to divinize them. Instead of becoming a god that will be sacrificed, these people become demonic. They take on sins of the community and personify these in the form of demonic possession. The sacrificial sequence has to proceed. The sins/impurities need to be expelled from the community and someone needs to be killed/sacrificed in order to destroy the cache of sin and impurity built up by the community and now personified in the possessed. Exorcism destroys the demon by expelling it from the possessed. That is why I believe the rite of exorcism must embody echoes or elements of the sacrificial rite for it to be effective. The demon needs to be killed, destroyed, or expelled along with all his impurities. Thus, we should expect the rite of exorcism to contain traces of the sacrifice of the (impure) king/scapegoat.

It should be noted that the ancient rite of exorcism was recently (in 1999) revised by a commission within the Church. The revised rite of exorcism, which replaces Pope Leo XIII's version of 1614, consists of about 90 pages of instructions and recitations. Its basic structure is very simple. There is a recitation of the litany of saints, a Gospel reading, a homily, and then supplications to God to bless the possessed as well as a set of commands to the demon to leave the possessed. The preparatory acts, such as the invocation of the saints and other supernatural beings, makes sense if this is going to be a sacrifice. To destroy/expel a supernatural being who is filled with the evil produced by a whole people or community, power is needed. Supernatural power comes from supernatural beings so they must be asked for help. We will see that it matters who is asked for help. The exorcist also gathers his powers in myriad other ways, as well as we will see below.

After these preparatory rites the exorcist reads aloud from the Holy Scriptures and then asks God to bless the possessed. This makes sense if what is happening is a sacrifice. If the victim has to carry the impurities of the community he has to be made into a supernatural being; he has to be divinized or supernaturalized. This is accomplished via reading passages from the holy scriptures that describe the process of incarnation or divinization and it is done by having God bless the victim. Exsufflation or breathing onto the victim also supernaturalizes the victim. Breathing on the other was an ancient way to impart the spirit to others, thus facilitating their spirit possession. Jesus did this with his apostles. He breathed on them, saying "Receive the holy spirit." Laying on of hands accomplishes the same aim of supernaturalizing the victim by imparting spirit. There are other ways to prepare the victim as well but they are all intended to supernaturalize the victim before the victim is sacrificed or destroyed. Only a god or a supernatural being can carry the weight of the sins of the community so it is necessary to make sure the victim is made into a god before that victim is killed. Once the preparatory acts are completed then the exorcism itself is done and this is equivalent to the blood sacrifice as it expels or destroys the demon.

PREPARATORY INSTRUCTIONS

The exorcist has to be a priest of learning and good reputation. He has to obtain permission from his local bishop to perform the exorcism and he has to take steps to ensure that any mental illness afflicting the "patient" is addressed by competent medical doctors. Exorcists are instructed to look for signs of genuine diabolical obsession/possession. These are: speaking in foreign or ancient tongues, clairvoyance or revealing distant or hidden things; displaying extraordinary physical strength, and an intense aversion to the things of God. Note that all of these signs make sense if the point of the whole exercise is a sacrifice or killing of a supernatural being. First, we need to make sure that the victim is indeed a god or a supernatural being as only a supernatural being can carry the sins of the community and the whole point of killing the god is to kill or destroy all the sins along with the god. So we need to establish the fact that we are really dealing here with a supernatural being. Speaking foreign or ancient languages, paranormal mental and physical abilities, and an intense aversion to goodness all establish the fact that we are dealing with a supernaturally evil being.

Let us now follow the ritual more closely to demonstrate its sacrificial structure:

RITE OF EXORCISM

The priest delegated by the Ordinary to perform this office should first go to confession or at least elicit an act of contrition, and, if convenient, offer the holy Sacrifice of the Mass, and implore God's help in other fervent prayers.

Comment: The exorcist needs to gather supernatural power in order to invest the victim with that power. Investing the victim will supernaturalize the victim thus making him suitable for sacrifice.

He vests in surplice and purple stole.

Comment: Surplice and purple stole are vestments that were originally used to keep one's person pure and clean. The priest will later in the ritual touch the purple stole to the victim's body. This again can be interpreted as an act that supernaturalizes, purifies, the victim in preparation for sacrifice. The fact that a purple stole is used recalls the royal origins of sacrifice—purple has always been the color of royalty in the West.

Having before him the person possessed (who should be bound if there is any danger), he traces the sign of the cross over him, over himself, and the bystanders, and then sprinkles all of them with holy water.

Comment: Holy water is water and salt blessed by an authorized sacred person. Salt was used by the ancient people of the Near East to protect against demons. It was thrown behind the body to ward off demons and placed in strategic sections of a house and so on. Tracing the sign of the cross and sprinkling of holy water on the victim once again supernaturalizes the victim.

   After this he kneels and says the Litany of the Saints, exclusive of the prayers which follow it. All present are to make the responses.

Comment: Recitation of these litanies indicates that the exorcist is recruiting power, supernatural power. But interestingly he does not recruit power indiscriminately. He calls on only certain supernatural beings, not all beings. He begins with the Trinity and then descends down the hierarchy to Mary, the archangels, the apostles, the patriarchs and prophets, and then eventually he comes to the holy innocents, martyrs and virgins, and so on. Why these? These too were sacrificial victims. They were spotless, yet were killed. They carried the sins of their communities and died for their people like the kings of old. The power that the exorcist gathers from all his pleas for help will be used to supernaturalize the victim, to identify the demon and then destroy the demon.

LITANY OF THE SAINTS

P: Lord, have mercy.
All: Lord, have mercy.
P: Christ, have mercy.
All: Christ, have mercy.
P: Lord, have mercy.
All: Lord, have mercy.
P: Christ, hear us.
All: Christ, graciously hear us.
P: God, the Father in heaven.
All: Have mercy on us.
P: God, the Son, Redeemer of the world.
All: Have mercy on us.
P: God, the Holy Spirit.
All: Have mercy on us.
P: Holy Trinity, one God.
All: Have mercy on us.
Holy Mary, pray for us,*
   * After each invocation: "Pray for us."

Holy Mother of God,
Holy Virgin of virgins,
St. Michael,
St. Gabriel,
St. Raphael,
All holy angels and archangels,
All holy orders of blessed spirits,
St. John the Baptist,
St. Joseph,
All holy patriarchs and prophets,
St. Peter,
St. Paul,
St. Andrew,
St. James,
St. John,
St. Thomas,
St. James,
St. Philip,
St. Bartholomew,
St. Matthew,
St. Simon,
St. Thaddeus,
St. Matthias,
St. Barnabas,
St. Luke,
St. Mark,
All holy apostles and evangelists,
All holy disciples of the Lord,
All holy Innocents,
St. Stephen,
St. Lawrence,
St. Vincent,
SS. Fabian and Sebastian,
SS. John and Paul,
SS. Cosmas and Damian,
SS. Gervase and Protase,
All holy martyrs,
St. Sylvester,
St. Gregory,
St. Ambrose,
St. Augustine,

St. Jerome,
St. Martin,
St. Nicholas,
All holy bishops and confessors,
All holy doctors,
St. Anthony,
St. Benedict,
St. Bernard,
St. Dominic,
St. Francis,
All holy priests and levites,
All holy monks and hermits,
St. Mary Magdalen,
St. Agatha,
St. Lucy,
St. Agnes,
St. Cecilia,
St. Catherine,
St. Anastasia,
All holy virgins and widows,
P: All holy saints of God,
All: Intercede for us.
P: Be merciful,
All: Spare us, O Lord.
P: Be merciful,
All: Graciously hear us, O Lord.

Comment: After receiving all these powers from God and other supernatural beings the exorcist then lists the catalog of impurities that is being carried by the possessed and embodied in the demon. These are the impurities and evils that the community wants to get rid of and that need to be destroyed via the sacrificial rite:

From all evil, deliver us, O Lord.*
    * After each invocation: "Deliver us, O Lord."
From all sin,
From your wrath,
From sudden and unprovided death,
From the snares of the devil,
From anger, hatred, and all ill will,
From all lewdness,

From lightning and tempest,
From the scourge of earthquakes,
From plague, famine, and war,
From everlasting death,

Comment: After the pleas for help from the saints and martyrs and the hierarchy of supernatural beings and after listing the evils that need to be destroyed, the exorcist returns to pleading for power. This time the exorcist directly asks God for all kinds of extraordinary powers. He begins by witnessing to the extraordinary concern God has for human beings and then directly asks God for power:

By the mystery of your holy incarnation,
By your coming,
By your birth,
By your baptism and holy fasting,
By your cross and passion,
By your death and burial,
By your holy resurrection,
By your wondrous ascension,
By the coming of the Holy,
Spirit, the Advocate,
On the day of judgment,
P: We sinners,
All: We beg you to hear us.*
    * After each invocation: "We beg you to hear us."
That you spare us,
That you pardon us,
That you bring us to true penance,
That you govern and preserve your holy Church,
That you preserve our Holy Father
and all ranks in the Church in holy religion,
That you humble the enemies of holy Church,
That you give peace and true concord to all Christian rulers.
That you give peace and unity to the whole Christian world,
That you restore to the unity of the Church all who have strayed
    from the truth, and lead all unbelievers to the light of the Gospel,
That you confirm and preserve us in your holy service,
That you lift up our minds to heavenly desires,
That you grant everlasting blessings to all our benefactors,

That you deliver our souls and the souls of our brethren, relatives, and benefactors from everlasting damnation,

That you give and preserve the fruits of the earth,

That you grant eternal rest to all the faithful departed,

That you graciously hear us,

Son of God,

At the end of the litany he (the priest) adds the following:

P: Antiphon: Do not keep in mind, O Lord, our offenses or those of our parents, nor take vengeance on our sins.

P: Our Father who are in heaven, hallowed be thy name; thy kingdom come; thy will be done on earth as it is in heaven. Give us this day our daily bread; and forgive us our trespasses as we forgive those who trespass against us; and lead us not into temptation,

All: But deliver us from evil.

Comment: Up to this moment in the ritual the exorcist has been speaking in his own name. But now he begins to adopt the kingly voice. He does this by reciting a psalm. The Psalms were either written (sung) by King David himself or were written as part of royal ceremonies—generally, ceremonies that involved the king presiding over the sacrifice. In this Psalm the king explicitly says that he will freely offer Yahweh the sacrifice. Thus, the recitation of a psalm is fitting at this point in the sacrifice/exorcism. The exorcist has gathered supernatural power. He therefore needs to speak with a voice of power and kingly authority. The royal songs we call the Psalms are suitable vehicles for this voice.

Psalm 53

P: God, by your name save me, and by your might defend my cause.

All: God, hear my prayer; hearken to the words of my mouth.

P: For haughty men have risen up against me, and fierce men seek my life; they set not God before their eyes.

All: See, God is my helper; the Lord sustains my life.

P: Turn back the evil upon my foes; in your faithfulness destroy them.

All: Freely will I offer you sacrifice; I will praise your name, Lord, for its goodness,

P: Because from all distress you have rescued me, and my eyes look down upon my enemies.

All: Glory be to the Father.
P: As it was in the beginning.

After the psalm the priest continues:
P: Save your servant.
All: Who trusts in you, my God.
P: Let him (her) find in you, Lord, a fortified tower.
All: In the face of the enemy.
P: Let the enemy have no power over him (her).
All: And the son of iniquity be powerless to harm him (her).
P: Lord, send him (her) aid from your holy place.
All: And watch over him (her) from Sion.
P: Lord, heed my prayer.
All: And let my cry be heard by you.
P: The Lord be with you.
All: May He also be with you.

Comment: At this point in the ritual we are getting close to the time when the victim needs to be supernaturalized or made into a supernatural being so that he can carry the evil of the community and so that he can along with all the evil he carries be sacrificially destroyed. The victim needs to be made "pure" before he can carry all the impurities of the community. Thus a request is made to "pardon" or purify the victim and then the exorcist launches into a prayer where he begins to characterize the demon. The demon is the beast, the dragon of old. Note that these sort of images once again call up the kingly theme in sacrifice. Mythologically speaking, kings in the West became kings by slaying a dragon.

Let us pray.

    God, whose nature is ever merciful and forgiving, accept our prayer that this servant of yours, bound by the fetters of sin, may be pardoned by your loving kindness.

    Holy Lord, almighty Father, everlasting God and Father of our Lord Jesus Christ, who once and for all consigned that fallen and apostate tyrant to the flames of hell, who sent your only-begotten Son into the world to crush that roaring lion; hasten to our call for help and snatch from ruination and from the clutches of the noonday devil this human being made in your image and likeness. Strike terror, Lord, into the beast now laying waste your vineyard. Fill your servants with courage to fight manfully against that reprobate dragon, lest he despise those who put their trust in you, and say with Pharaoh of old: "I know not God, nor will I set Israel free." Let your

mighty hand cast him out of your servant, (The name of the person), so he may no longer hold captive this person whom it pleased you to make in your image, and to redeem through your Son; who lives and reigns with you, in the unity of the Holy Spirit, God, forever and ever.
All: Amen.

Comment: At this point in the ritual the cast of characters have now been assembled and properly prepared and characterized. If we are going to perform a sacrificial rite then we need a supernaturalized victim and an empowered king who performs the sacrifice. We can then expect an initial foray into the mytheme called "the king slaying the dragon." I do not intend to speak lightly or disrespectfully here of the roles of the participants in this drama. The drama is real, the suffering is real, the efforts of the exorcist heroic and compassionate. I merely am trying to indicate that the drama draws some of its ritual efficacy by recalling very ancient sacrificial and mythological themes.

Then he commands the demon as follows:
I command you, unclean spirit, whoever you are, along with all your minions now attacking this servant of God, by the mysteries of the incarnation, passion, resurrection, and ascension of our Lord Jesus Christ, by the descent of the Holy Spirit, by the coming of our Lord for judgment, that you tell me by some sign your name, and the day and hour of your departure.

Comment: This is a turning point in the ritual. As we have seen in previous chapters of this work the elicitation of the name of the demon indicates a gaining of control over the demon. All the ancient cultures of the Near East believed in the power of name to capture the essence or spirit of an entity. Knowing the name of a spirit allowed one to control that spirit. The exorcist has gathered his powers and he now uses it to control the demon. He wants the name and the time of departure. Getting the name of the demon completes the process of supernaturalizing the victim. It crystallizes the supernatural nature that carries the sins of the people. We now know who will be destroyed (and when).

I command you, moreover, to obey me to the letter, I who am a minister of God despite my unworthiness; nor shall you be emboldened to harm in any way this creature of God, or the bystanders, or any of their possessions.

The priest lays his hand on the head of the sick person,

Comment: We finally come to the laying on of hands ritual. The "laying on of hands" was used by the early Christians to expel demons but Jesus seemed to use the ritual to heal people rather than to exorcize demons per se. He usually exorcized via command (after obtaining the name of the demon). The apostles used the ritual to pass on authority or power to others in the line of succession (to confirm a person as Christian or to create a bishop and so forth). The laying on of hands ritual was also sometimes used in the anointing of kings. Its basic structure is the passing on of supernatural power from the hands of the priest to the person receiving the blessing. Thus this laying on of hands completes the supernaturalizing process in this sacrificial rite. Alternatively the laying of hands attempts to replace the evil spirit with a holy spirit. It uses power to cast out the demon. It is the exorcism. In this case it constitutes the sacrifice itself, saying:

They shall lay their hands upon the sick and all will be well with them. May Jesus, Son of Mary, Lord and Savior of the world, through the merits and intercession of His holy apostles Peter and Paul and all His saints, show you favor and mercy.
All: Amen.

Comment: I am inclined to think that the laying on of hands ritual is part of the supernaturalizing process because just after it we get a series of gospel readings that are all about the supernaturalizing process as exemplified by the case of Jesus. In Jesus' case he manifests divinity via the incarnation and via his life and works. Thus the exorcist reads those gospel passages that speak to the issue of the incarnation and divinization. Then another blessing and sprinkling of holy water on the victim—once again these actions are consistent with the effort to supernaturalize/purify the victim in preparation for sacrifice.

Next he reads over the possessed person these selections from the Gospel, or at least one of them.

P: The Lord be with you.
All: May He also be with you.
P: The beginning of the holy Gospel according to St. John.
All: Glory be to you, O Lord.

A Lesson from the Holy Gospel according to St. John
(John 1:1–14)

As he says these opening words he signs himself and the possessed on the brow, lips, and breast.

> When time began, the Word was there, and the Word was face to face with God, and the Word was God. This Word, when time began, was face to face with God. All things came into being through Him, and without Him there came to be not one thing that has come to be. In Him was life, and the life was the light of men. The light shines in the darkness, and the darkness did not lay hold of it. There came upon the scene a man, a messenger from God, whose name was John. This man came to give testimony to testify in behalf of the light that all might believe through him. He was not himself the light; he only was to testify in behalf of the light. Meanwhile the true light, which illumines every man, was making its entrance into the world. He was in the world, and the world came to be through Him, and the world did not acknowledge Him. He came into His home, and His own people did not welcome Him. But to as many as welcomed Him He gave the power to become children of God those who believe in His name; who were born not of blood, or of carnal desire, or of man's will; no, they were born of God. (Genuflect here.) And the Word became man and lived among us; and we have looked upon His glory such a glory as befits the Father's only-begotten Son full of grace and truth!
> All: Thanks be to God.

Lastly he blesses the sick person, saying:

> May the blessing of almighty God,
> Father, Son, and Holy Spirit,
> come upon you and remain with you forever.
> All: Amen.

Then he sprinkles the person with holy water.

A Lesson from the Holy Gospel according to St. Mark
(Mark 16:15–18)

> At that time Jesus said to His disciples: "Go into the whole world and preach the Gospel to all creation. He that believes and is baptized will be saved; he that does not believe will be condemned. And

in the way of proofs of their claims, the following will accompany those who believe: in my name they will drive out demons; they will speak in new tongues; they will take up serpents in their hands, and if they drink something deadly, it will not hurt them; they will lay their hands on the sick, and these will recover."

A Lesson from the Holy Gospel according to St. Luke
(Luke 10:17–20)

At that time the seventy-two returned in high spirits. "Master," they said, "even the demons are subject to us because we use your name!" "Yes," He said to them, "I was watching Satan fall like lightning that flashes from heaven. But mind: it is I that have given you the power to tread upon serpents and scorpions, and break the dominion of the enemy everywhere; nothing at all can injure you. Just the same, do not rejoice in the fact that the spirits are subject to you, but rejoice in the fact that your names are engraved in heaven."

A Lesson from the Holy Gospel according to St. Luke
(Luke 11:14–22)

At that time Jesus was driving out a demon, and this particular demon was dumb. The demon was driven out, the dumb man spoke, and the crowds were enraptured. But some among the people remarked: "He is a tool of Beelzebul, and that is how he drives out demons!" Another group, intending to test Him, demanded of Him a proof of His claims, to be shown in the sky. He knew their inmost thoughts. "Any kingdom torn by civil strife," He said to them, "is laid in ruins; and house tumbles upon house. So, too, if Satan is in revolt against himself, how can his kingdom last, since you say that I drive out demons as a tool of Beelzebul. And furthermore: if I drive out demons as a tool of Beelzebul, whose tools are your pupils when they do the driving out? Therefore, judged by them, you must stand condemned. But, if, on the contrary, I drive out demons by the finger of God, then, evidently the kingdom of God has by this time made its way to you. As long as a mighty lord in full armor guards his premises, he is in peaceful possession of his property; but should one mightier than he attack and overcome him, he will strip him of his armor, on which he had relied, and distribute the spoils taken from him."

P: Lord, heed my prayer.
All: And let my cry be heard by you.

Comment: These latter gospel passages recall Jesus' status as King and Messiah, One who has authority to perform the sacrificial rites. Jesus cites his ability to cast out demons, that is, to perform the sacrifices as proof of his royal status and the coming of his kingdom. The recitation of these gospel passages at this point in the rite seems to be indicating that enactment of a sacrifice is proper and legitimate . . . and will be effective given that it is in the name of the King Jesus. Jesus delegates his royal authority to perform the sacrifice to his apostles. The citing of the source of the authority to perform the blood sacrifice usually comes just before the sacrifice itself, so we can expect the moment of sacrifice, the destruction of the demon, is coming soon.

> P: The Lord be with you.
> All: May He also be with you.
> Let us pray.
>   Almighty Lord, Word of God the Father, Jesus Christ, God and Lord of all creation; who gave to your holy apostles the power to tramp underfoot serpents and scorpions; who along with the other mandates to work miracles was pleased to grant them the authority to say: "Depart, you devils!" and by whose might Satan was made to fall from heaven like lightning; I humbly call on your holy name in fear and trembling, asking that you grant me, your unworthy servant, pardon for all my sins, steadfast faith, and the power—supported by your mighty arm—to confront with confidence and resolution this cruel demon. I ask this through you, Jesus Christ, our Lord and God, who are coming to judge both the living and the dead and the world by fire.
> All: Amen.

Comment: We have finally come to the moment of sacrifice, of exorcism. All the component rituals that are part of the whole are now gathered together and performed simultaneously: The rituals to purify the victim (the sign of the cross, the touching of the stole to the neck, the laying on of hands, etc.) and the ritual exorcism itself:

> Next he makes the sign of the cross over himself and the one possessed, places the end of the stole on the latter's neck, and, putting his right hand on the latter's head, he says the following in accents filled with confidence and faith:
> P: See the cross of the Lord; begone, you hostile powers!
> All: The stem of David, the lion of Juda's tribe has conquered.

Comment: Kingly authority (stem of David, Lion of Judah, and so on) is invoked. The king is effectively performing the sacrifice.

P: Lord, heed my prayer.
All: And let my cry be heard by you.
P: The Lord be with you.
All: May He also be with you.
Let us pray.
    God and Father of our Lord Jesus Christ, I appeal to your holy name, humbly begging your kindness, that you graciously grant me help against this and every unclean spirit now tormenting this creature of yours; through Christ our Lord.
All: Amen.

Exorcism

I cast you out, unclean spirit, along with every Satanic power of the enemy, every spectre from hell, and all your fell companions; in the name of our Lord Jesus + Christ. Begone and stay far from this creature of God. + For it is He who commands you, He who flung you headlong from the heights of heaven into the depths of hell. It is He who commands you, He who once stilled the sea and the wind and the storm. Hearken, therefore, and tremble in fear, Satan, you enemy of the faith, you foe of the human race, you begetter of death, you robber of life, you corrupter of justice, you root of all evil and vice; seducer of men, betrayer of the nations, instigator of envy, font of avarice, fomentor of discord, author of pain and sorrow. Why, then, do you stand and resist, knowing as you must that Christ the Lord brings your plans to nothing? Fear Him, who in Isaac was offered in sacrifice, in Joseph sold into bondage, slain as the paschal lamb, crucified as man, yet triumphed over the powers of hell. (The three signs of the cross which follow are traced on the brow of the possessed person). Begone, then, in the name of the Father, + and of the Son, + and of the Holy + Spirit. Give place to the Holy Spirit by this sign of the holy + cross of our Lord Jesus Christ, who lives and reigns with the Father and the Holy Spirit, God, forever and ever.
All: Amen.

Comment: The above ritual text brings the sacrifice into full view. The victim/demon is ritually slaughtered with overwhelming power. The sign of the cross traced three times on the forehead of the victim translates the massive power of the imagery used in the text into an experience within the body of the victim. But all this is just the opening salvo. We will need two more ritual slayings of the demon to complete the expulsion. Each of the three, however, has a special purpose. This first one transfers power into the body of the possessed and against the person of the demon. It begins the expulsion process.

P: Lord, heed my prayer.
All: And let my cry be heard by you.
P: The Lord be with you.
All: May He also be with you.
Let us pray.

God, Creator and defender of the human race, who made man in your own image, look down in pity on this your servant, N., now in the toils of the unclean spirit, now caught up in the fearsome threats of man's ancient enemy, sworn foe of our race, who befuddles and stupefies the human mind, throws it into terror, overwhelms it with fear and panic. Repel, O Lord, the devil's power, break asunder his snares and traps, put the unholy tempter to flight. By the sign + (on the brow) of your name, let your servant be protected in mind and body. (The three crosses which follow are traced on the breast of the possessed person). Keep watch over the inmost recesses of his (her) + heart; rule over his (her) + emotions; strengthen his (her) + will. Let vanish from his (her) soul the temptings of the mighty adversary. Graciously grant, O Lord, as we call on your holy name, that the evil spirit, who hitherto terrorized over us, may himself retreat in terror and defeat, so that this servant of yours may sincerely and steadfastly render you the service which is your due; through Christ our Lord.
All: Amen.

Comment: Next comes the second step in the expulsion process. Given that this is a sacrifice designed to rid the community of its sins and impurities the community needs to explicitly reject those impurities so we need a formal adjuration or command from the community (in the person of the exorcist speaking with authority) to the demon to depart. The adjuration is repeated and with every greater force until once again we get the royal imagery of the king slaying the dragon. But the theme here is command to depart. The separation of the pure and impure. The contrasts of pure and impure and the expulsion of the impure.

Exorcism

I adjure you, ancient serpent, by the judge of the living and the dead, by your Creator, by the Creator of the whole universe, by Him who has the power to consign you to hell, to depart forthwith in fear, along with your savage minions, from this servant of God, N., who seeks refuge in the fold of the Church. I adjure you again, + (on the brow) not by my weakness but by the might of the Holy Spirit, to depart from this servant of God, N., whom almighty God has made in His image. Yield, therefore, yield not to my own person but to the minister of Christ. For it is the power of Christ that compels you, who brought you low by His cross. Tremble before that mighty arm that broke asunder the dark prison walls and led souls forth to light. May the trembling that afflicts this human frame, + (on the breast) the fear that afflicts this image + (on the brow) of God, descend on you. Make no resistance nor delay in departing from this man, for it has pleased Christ to dwell in man. Do not think of despising my command because you know me to be a great sinner. It is God + Himself who commands you; the majestic Christ + who commands you. God the Father + commands you; God the Son + commands you; God the Holy + Spirit commands you. The mystery of the cross commands + you. The faith of the holy apostles Peter and Paul and of all the saints commands ı you. The blood of the martyrs commands + you. The continence of the confessors commands + you. The devout prayers of all holy men and women command + you. The saving mysteries of our Christian faith command + you.

Depart, then, transgressor. Depart, seducer, full of lies and cunning, foe of virtue, persecutor of the innocent. Give place, abominable creature, give way, you monster, give way to Christ, in whom you found none of your works. For He has already stripped you of your powers and laid waste your kingdom, bound you prisoner and plundered your weapons. He has cast you forth into the outer darkness, where everlasting ruin awaits you and your abettors. To what purpose do you insolently resist? To what purpose do you brazenly refuse? For you are guilty before almighty God, whose laws you have transgressed. You are guilty before His Son, our Lord Jesus Christ, whom you presumed to tempt, whom you dared to nail to the cross. You are guilty before the whole human race, to whom you proferred by your enticements the poisoned cup of death.

Therefore, I adjure you, profligate dragon, in the name of the spotless + Lamb, who has trodden down the asp and the basilisk, and overcome the lion and the dragon, to depart from this man (woman) + (on the brow), to depart from the Church of God + (signing the bystanders). Tremble and flee, as we call on the name of the Lord, before whom the denizens of hell cower, to whom the heavenly Virtues and Powers and Dominations are subject, whom the Cherubim and Seraphim praise with unending cries as they sing: Holy, holy, holy, Lord God of Sabaoth. The Word made flesh + commands you; the Virgin's Son + commands you; Jesus + of Nazareth commands you, who once, when you despised His disciples, forced you to flee in shameful defeat from a man; and when He had cast you out you did not even dare, except by His leave, to enter into a herd of swine. And now as I adjure you in His + name, begone from this man (woman) who is His creature. It is futile to resist His + will. It is hard for you to kick against the + goad. The longer you delay, the heavier your punishment shall be; for it is not men you are condemning, but rather Him who rules the living and the dead, who is coming to judge both the living and the dead and the world by fire.

All: Amen.
P: Lord, heed my prayer.
All: And let my cry be heard by you.
P: The Lord be with you.
All: May He also be with you.
Let us pray.

God of heaven and earth, God of the angels and archangels, God of the prophets and apostles, God of the martyrs and virgins, God who has power to bestow life after death and rest after toil; for there is no other God than you, nor can there be another true God beside you, the Creator of heaven and earth, who are truly a King, whose kingdom is without end; I humbly entreat your glorious majesty to deliver this servant of yours from the unclean spirits; through Christ our Lord.
All: Amen.

Comment: We finally come to the third and final set of adjurations and the final expulsion ritual.

Exorcism

Therefore, I adjure you every unclean spirit, every spectre from hell, every satanic power, in the name of Jesus + Christ of Nazareth, who was led into the desert after His baptism by John to vanquish you in your citadel, to cease your assaults against the creature whom He has, formed from the slime of the earth for His own honor and glory; to quail before wretched man, seeing in him the image of almighty God, rather than his state of human frailty. Yield then to God, + who by His servant, Moses, cast you and your malice, in the person of Pharaoh and his army, into the depths of the sea. Yield to God, + who, by the singing of holy canticles on the part of David, His faithful servant, banished you from the heart of King Saul. Yield to God, + who condemned you in the person of Judas Iscariot, the traitor. For He now flails you with His divine scourges, + He in whose sight you and your legions once cried out: "What have we to do with you, Jesus, Son of the Most High God? Have you come to torture us before the time?" Now He is driving you back into the everlasting fire, He who at the end of time will say to the wicked: "Depart from me, you accursed, into the everlasting fire which has been prepared for the devil and his angels." For you, O evil one, and for your followers there will be worms that never die. An unquenchable fire stands ready for you and for your minions, you prince of accursed murderers, father of lechery, instigator of sacrileges, model of vileness, promoter of heresies, inventor of every obscenity.

Depart, then, + impious one, depart, + accursed one, depart with all your deceits, for God has willed that man should be His temple. Why do you still linger here? Give honor to God the Father + almighty, before whom every knee must bow. Give place to the Lord Jesus + Christ, who shed His most precious blood for man. Give place to the Holy + Spirit, who by His blessed apostle Peter openly struck you down in the person of Simon Magus; who cursed your lies in Annas and Saphira; who smote you in King Herod because he had not given honor to God; who by His apostle Paul afflicted you with the night of blindness in the magician Elyma, and by the mouth of the same apostle bade you to go out of Pythonissa, the soothsayer. Begone, + now! Begone, + seducer! Your place is in solitude; your abode is in the nest of serpents; get down and crawl with them. This matter brooks no delay; for see, the Lord, the ruler comes quickly, kindling fire before Him, and it will run on ahead of Him and encompass His enemies in flames. You might delude man, but God you cannot mock. It is He who casts you out, from whose sight nothing is hidden. It is He who repels you, to whose might all things are subject. It is He who expels you, He who has prepared everlasting hellfire for you and your angels, from whose mouth shall come a sharp sword, who is coming to judge both the living and the dead and the world by fire.

All: Amen.

All the above may be repeated as long as necessary, until the one possessed has been fully freed.

Comment: The sacrifice has been performed. The demon has been ritually killed or expelled. Has the patient recovered? If not, the following prayers, which are the workhorses of the Catholic Church, are recommended. Note the royal theme throughout these prayers. The story of the Magi who came from the east to witness to the true nature of Jesus is really about witnessing to Jesus' kingly nature. The Magi brought gifts that were traditional gifts for a king. Similarly, the Magnificat is the kind of song the lady-in-waiting or the queen herself would sing for their king. These are songs about "regal nuptials." Zachary's canticle is an explicit recognition of the kingly status of Jesus. Why does the Catholic Church, at an exorcism, recommend that its exorcist recite all these prayers testifying to the kingly status of Jesus? It makes some sense if we see the rite of exorcism as recalling the ancient sacrificial rites and these ancient sacrificial rites in turn were based on the sacrifices performed by (and sometimes on) kings. The exorcist gets his authority to perform the sacrifice because he acts in the name of King Jesus.

It will also help to say devoutly and often over the afflicted person the Our Father, Hail Mary, and the Creed, as well as any of the prayers given below.

The Canticle of Our Lady, with the doxology; the Canticle of Zachary, with the doxology.

P: Antiphon: Magi from the East came to Bethlehem to adore the Lord; and opening their treasure chests they presented Him with precious gifts: Gold for the great King, incense for the true God, and myrrh in symbol of His burial. Alleluia.

Canticle of Our Lady (The Magnificat) (Luke 1:46–55)

P: My soul extols the Lord;

All: And my spirit leaps for joy in God my Savior.

P: How graciously He looked upon His lowly maid! Oh, see, from this hour onward age after age will call me blessed!

All: How sublime is what He has done for me, the Mighty One, whose name is "Holy"!

P: From age to age He visits those who worship Him in reverence.

All: His arm achieves the mastery: He routs the haughty and proud of heart.

P: He puts down princes from their thrones, and exalts the lowly;

All: He fills the hungry with blessings, and sends away the rich with empty hands.

P: He has taken by the hand His servant Israel, and mercifully kept His faith,

All: As He had promised our fathers with Abraham and his posterity forever and evermore.

P: Glory be to the Father.

All: As it was in the beginning.

Antiphon: Magi from the East came to Bethlehem to adore the Lord; and opening their treasure chests they presented Him with precious gifts: Gold for the great King, incense for the true God, and myrrh in symbol of His burial. Alleluia.

Meanwhile the home is sprinkled with holy water and incensed. Then the priest says:

P: Our Father who art in Heaven, Hallowed be Thy Name; Thy Kingdom come; Thy will be done on earth As it is in Heaven. Give us this day our daily bread; and forgive us our trespasses as we forgive those who trespass against us, and lead us not into temptation.

All: But deliver us from evil.

P: Many shall come from Saba.

All: Bearing gold and incense.

P: Lord, heed my prayer.

All: And let my cry be heard by you.

P: The Lord be with you.

All: May he also be with you.

Let us pray.

   God, who on this day revealed your only-begotten Son to all nations by the guidance of a star, grant that we who now know you by faith may finally behold you in your heavenly majesty; through Christ our Lord.

All: Amen.

Responsory: Be enlightened and shine forth, O Jerusalem, for your light is come; and upon you is risen the glory of the Lord Jesus Christ born of the Virgin Mary.

P: Nations shall walk in your light, and kings in the splendor of your birth.

All: And the glory of the Lord is risen upon you.

Let us pray.

Lord God almighty, bless + this home, and under its shelter let there be health, chastity, self-conquest, humility, goodness, mildness, obedience to your commandments, and thanksgiving to God the Father, Son, and Holy Spirit. May your blessing remain always in this home and on those who live here; through Christ our Lord.

All: Amen.

P: Antiphon for Canticle of Zachary: Today the Church is espoused to her heavenly bridegroom, for Christ washes her sins in the Jordan; the Magi hasten with gifts to the regal nuptials; and the guests are gladdened with water made wine, alleluia.

Canticle of Zachary (Luke 1:68–79)

P: Blessed be the Lord, the God of Israel! He has visited His people and brought about its redemption.

All: He has raised for us a stronghold of salvation in the house of David His servant,

P: And redeemed the promise He had made through the mouth of His holy prophets of old

All: To grant salvation from our foes and from the hand of all that hate us;

P: To deal in mercy with our fathers and be mindful of His holy covenant,

All: Of the oath he had sworn to our father Abraham, that He would enable us

P: Rescued from the clutches of our foes to worship Him without fear,

All: In holiness and observance of the Law, in His presence, all our days.

P: And you, my little one, will be hailed "Prophet of the Most High"; for the Lord's precursor you will be to prepare His ways;

All: You are to impart to His people knowledge of salvation through forgiveness of their sins.

P: Thanks be to the merciful heart of our God! a dawning Light from on high will visit us

All: To shine upon those who sit in darkness and in the shadowland of death, and guide our feet into the path of peace.

P: Glory be to the Father.

All: As it was in the beginning.

Antiphon: Today the Church is espoused to her heavenly bride-groom, for Christ washes her sins in the Jordan; the Magi hasten with gifts to the regal nuptials; and the guests are gladdened with water made wine, alleluia.

Then the celebrant sings:

P: The Lord be with you.

All: May He also be with you.

Let us pray.

   God, who on this day revealed your only-begotten Son to all nations by the guidance of a star, grant that we who now know you by faith may finally behold you in your heavenly majesty; through Christ our Lord.

All: Amen.

Comment: The Athanasian Creed is also sometimes recited as a sort of les-son in Catholic theology but essentially the exorcism rites, the sacrificial rites have now been completed. What remains is to end the sacrifice prop-erly, with kingly dignity. Some of the royal psalms may be recited but always a prayer of thanksgiving must be recited.

   P: Glory be to the Father

   All: As it was in the beginning.

Here follows a large number of psalms which may be used by the exorcist at his discretion but these are not a necessary part of the rite. Some of them occur in other parts of the ritual and are so indicated; the others may be taken from the Psalter. Psalm 90, 67, 69, 53, 117, 34, 30, 21, 3, 10, 12.

Prayer Following Deliverance

   P: Almighty God, we beg you to keep the evil spirit from fur-
         ther molesting this servant of yours, and to keep him far away,
         never to return. At your command, O Lord, may the goodness
         and peace of our Lord Jesus Christ, our Redeemer, take posses-
         sion of this man (woman). May we no longer fear any evil since
         the Lord is with us; who lives and reigns with you, in the unity
         of the Holy Spirit, God, forever and ever.

   All: Amen.

Chapter 11

Some Concluding Thoughts

The interpretation of the exorcism ritual and of demonic possession itself that I have offered here may not please all people but it is consistent with the larger theory of spirit possession-phenomena that I have laid out in this work. Spirit possession divinizes the possessed, at least temporarily. When possession is positive it enriches the life of the individual; when it is negative it diminishes the life of the individual. The focus of volume 2 has been on demonic forms of possession. In order to understand these horrifying instances of human suffering I have built on the findings of volume 1 to offer the following theory: Human society needs a way to order itself and human beings need a way to cooperate so as to attain to the good things of life. But cooperation is difficult because human beings are flawed and not completely trustworthy. We sin against one another and this creates discord and ultimately chaos.

Religion offered humanity the kingly sacrifice as a way to deal with the impurities and sins of communities. The idea was literal and simple: people created an exalted being who could contain or hold all the sins of the community and then they killed this being and along with him got rid of the sin. The exalted being had to be someone who could be seen and yet he could not be just any person. He had to somehow be special, physically spotless and spiritually blameless. That is why kings were created. They were above everyone else and yet they were connected to everyone else. Thus they were in a position to collect impurities from everyone. They were exalted, special, and awesome—yet they could also literally be seen. To further exalt the king people needed to make them into gods and spirit possession accomplished this task. Unlike ordinary people and the shamans of old, the kings could remain spirit possessed indefinitely. They in effect became gods. This divine status made them suitable for sacrifice because it meant that they could carry the most unimaginable power and evil.

The ritual killing of kings continued in premodern tribal societies right up to the modern era but the practice died out whenever the kings could convince the people that suitable substitutes could be procured. Any substitute created had to be sacred and exalted. That substitute had to be divinized before sacrificed. Again the reason for this was that only exalted beings could carry the weight of the community. The most reliable way to divinize these sacrificial victims was spirit possession. The proliferation of religious rituals around the historical development of the sacrificial rites constitutes the standard histories of religions. Everywhere the kings performed the most important rituals. But they also delegated much of the work to the priests. The priests in turn devised new ways to divinize the victims and to prepared them for sacrifice.

All this summarizes a vastly more complex story and reality than I can describe here. My point here is that at the heart of the religious experience is the sacrifice and the sacrifice is rooted in spirit possession and royal power. When the kings began to lose their religious significance demonic possession phenomena began to rise in frequency and intensity. When the kings or suitable substitutes can no longer embody the sins of the people, vulnerable people will attempt to do so. They become the victims in the sacrificial drama. They take on the sins of the community and personify these in the form of a demon. The demon can then be ritually sacrificed or destroyed and thus the sins of the community ritually expelled.

If I am correct in detecting echoes of the ancient sacrificial rites of humankind in the phenomena of demonic possession, then demonic possession needs to be treated ritually. Once mental illness is excluded, then the possessed should be free to choose ritual exorcism if their beliefs lead them there. Only the strong can take on the sins of their brethren and act as willing victims in a sacrifice. These people need to be respected, not merely pitied.

Ultimately, the most effective remedy for demonic possession is knowledge. Understanding its roots and its power will help us to develop effective remedies. But at its core is the mystery of sacrifice itself. Why did human beings hit on the idea of sacrifice as a method to organize social orders? The sacrifice was the central organizing principle of societies the world over for millennia and the kings embodied that order for an equally long stretch of time. What is the principle that confers order on societies today? And, who embodies the ordering principle now? Who speaks with the voice of the Divine One now? Who speaks with authority now? When the ancient sacrificial rites are no longer performed what do people do to maintain order? We appear to be doing fine without any overt system of sacrifice. Or are we?

References

Associated Press. 2009. Warning signs missed in baby mutilation case. July 28. http://www.msnbc.msn.com/id/32185637/ns/us_news-crime_and_courts// (accessed June 15, 2010).

Bastin, M.-L. 1984. Ritual masks of the Chokwe. *African Arts* 17 (4): 40–45, 92–93, 95–96.

Batson, C. D., P. Shoenrade, and W. L. Ventis. 1993. *Religion and the individual: A social-psychological perspective*. New York: Oxford University Press.

Bear, D. M., and P. Fedio. 1977. Quantitative analysis of interictal behavior in temporal lobe epilepsy. *Archives of Neurology* 34 (8): 454–467.

Blatty, W. P. 1971. *The exorcist*. New York: Harper and Row.

Boddy, J. 1989. *Wombs and alien spirits: Women, men, and the Zār Cult in Northern Sudan*. Madison: University of Wisconsin Press.

Brun, C. C., N. Leporé, E. Luders, Y. Y. Chou, S. K. Madsen, A. W. Toga, et al. 2009. Sex differences in brain structure in auditory and cingulated regions. *Neuro Report* 20 (10): 930–935.

Carrazana, E., J. DeToledo, R. Rivas-Vasquez, G. Rey, and S. Wheeler. 1999. Epilepsy and religious experiences: Voodoo possession. *Epilepsia* 40:239–241.

Cheyne, J. A. 1995. A webpage about sleep paralysis and associated hypnagogic and hypnopompic experiences. http://watarts.uwaterloo.ca/~acheyne/S_P.html (accessed June 16, 2010).

Collaer, M. L., S. Reimers, and J. T. Manning. 2007. Visuospatial performance on an internet line judgment task and potential hormonal markers: Sex, sexual orientation, and 2D:4D. *Archives of Sexual Behavior* 36 (2): 177–192.

Cosgrove, K. P., C. M. Mazure, and J. K. Staley. 2007. Evolving knowledge of sex differences in brain structure, function, and chemistry. *Biological Psychiatry* 62 (8): 847–855.

Curtis, M. Y., and R. Sarro. 1997. The "Nimba" headdress: Art, ritual, and history of the Baga and Nalu peoples of Guinea. *Art Institute of Chicago Museum Studies and African Art at the Art Institute of Chicago* 23 (2): 120–133, 196–197.

DePalatis, R. S. 2006. An exploration of the different responses to a deliverance ministry procedure: Possession trance and dissociation in the Protestant Christian expulsion ritual setting. Ph.D. diss., Capella University.

Devinsky, O., and G. Lai. 2008. Spirituality and religion in epilepsy. *Epilepsy and Behavior* 12 (4): 636–643.

Dietrich, A. 2004. Neurocognitive mechanisms underlying the experience of flow. *Consciousness and Cognition* 13 (4): 746–761.

The exorcist (film). 1973. Directed by W. Friedkin. Warner Bros. Pictures.

The exorcism of Emily Rose (film). 2005. Directed by S. Derrickson. Sony.

Finkel, D., and M. McGue. 1997. Sex differences and nonadditivity in heritability of the Multidimensional Personality Questionnaire Scales. *Journal of Personality and Social Psychology* 72 (4): 929–938.

Freud, S. 1913. *Totem and taboo.* New York: W. W. Norton.

Freud, S. 1923. A neurosis of demonical possession in the seventeenth century. Translated by J. Riviere. In *Collected papers*, 4:436–472. New York: Basic Books.

Freud, S. 1927. *The future of an illusion.* Translated by W. D. Robson-Scott. London: Hogarth Press.

Freud, S. 1930. *Civilization and its discontents.* New York: W. W. Norton.

Freud, S. 1938. *Moses and monotheism.* London: Hogarth Press.

Geschwind, N. 1979. Behavioural changes in temporal lobe epilepsy. *Psychological Medicine* 9: 217–219.

Green, R., and B. Keverne. 2000. The disparate maternal aunt-uncle ration in male transsexuals: An explanation invoking genomic imprinting. *Journal of Theoretical Biology* 202 (1): 55–63.

Haig, D. 2000. Genomic imprinting, sex-biased dispersal, and social behavior. *Annals of the New York Academy of Sciences* 907:149–163.

Haig, D. 2002. *Genomic imprinting and kinship.* New Brunswick, NJ: Rutgers University Press.

Haig, D., and M. Westoby. 1988. Inclusive fitness, seed resources and maternal care. In *Plant reproductive ecology*, ed. J. L. Doust, 60–79. New York: Oxford University Press.

Hufford, D. J. 1982. *The terror that comes in the night: An experience-centered study of supernatural assault traditions.* Philadelphia: University of Pennsylvania Press.

Huguelet, P., S. Mohr, L. Borras, C. Gilliéron, and P. Y. Brandt. 2006. Spirituality and religious practices among outpatients with schizophrenia and their clinicians. *Psychiatric Services* 57 (3): 366–372.

Isichei, E. 1988. On masks and audible ghosts: Some secret male cults in central Nigeria. *Journal of Religion in Africa* 18 (1): 42–70.

James VI. 1597/1969. *Daemonologie.* New York: De Capo Press.

James VI. 1598/1930. *True law of free monarchies.* Reprinted in J. R. Tanner, *Constitutional Documents of the Reign of James I 1602–1625.* Cambridge: Cambridge University Press.

Knight, C. 1991. *Blood relations: Menstruation and the origins of culture.* New Haven: Yale University Press.

Kramer, H., and J. Sprenger. 1487/1971. *Malleus maleficarum*. Edited and translated by M. Summers. New York: Dover.

Kua, E. H., L. P. Sim, and K. T. Chee. 1986. A cross-cultural study of the possession-trance in Singapore. *Australian and New Zealand Journal of Psychiatry* 20 (3): 361–364.

Laidlaw, T. M., D. Prabudha, N. Akira, and J. H. Gruzelier. 2005. Low self-directedness (TCI), mood, schizotypy and hypnotic susceptibility. *Personality and Individual Differences* 39 (2): 469–480.

Lalumière, M. L., R. Blanchard, and K. J. Zucker. 2000. Sexual orientation and handedness in men and women: A meta-analysis. *Psychological Bulletin* 126:575–592.

Le, C., J. Smith, and L. Cohen. 2009. Mirror writing and a dissociative identity disorder. *Case Reports in Medicine*, Article ID 814292, 2 pages.

Marinos, J. 1997. Laterality and dissociative identity disorder: Perceptual asymmetries in host and later identities on tests of dichotic listening and global-local processing. *Dissertation Abstract International* 58(08), p. 4506B (UMI No. 9806868). Retrieved June 15, 2010, from Dissertations and Theses database.

Mather, C. 1689. *Memorable providences relating to witchcrafts and possessions*. Boston: R. P.

McNamara, P. 2008. *Nightmares: The science and solution of those frightening visions during sleep*. Westport, CT: Praeger Perspectives.

McNamara, P. 2009. *The neuroscience of religious experience*. New York: Cambridge University Press.

Mohr, S., P. Y. Brandt, L. Borras, C. Gilliéron, and P. Huguelet. 2006. Toward an integration of spirituality and religiousness into the psychosocial dimension of schizophrenia. *American Journal of Psychiatry* 163 (11): 1952–1959.

Nakamura, J., and M. Csikszentmihalyi. 2005. The concept of flow. In *Handbook of positive psychology*, ed. C. R. Snyder and S. J. Lopez, 89–105. New York: Oxford University Press.

The Nightmare Project. www.nightmareproject.com (no longer accessible after December 2007).

Oesterreich, T. K. 1922/1974. *Possession and exorcism among primitive races, in antiquity, the Middle Ages, and modern times*. New York: Causeway Books.

Ott, U., M. Reuter, J. Hennig, and D. Vaitl. 2005. Evidence for the common biological basis of the absorption trait, hallucinogen effects, and positive symptoms: Epistasis between 5-HT2a and COMT polymorphisms. *America Journal of Medical Genetics Part B* 137B:29–32.

Prohaska, P. R. 2002. Religious beliefs and trait absorption scores: Implications for mental and physical health. *Dissertation Abstracts International, 62* (10), 4459–B. Retrieved June 15, 2010, from Dissertations and Theses database.

Ramachandran, V. S., and S. Blakeslee. 1998. *Phantoms in the brain: Probing the mysteries of the human mind*. New York: William Morrow.

Ross, J., D. Roeltgen, and A. Zinn. 2006. Cognition and the sex chromosomes: Studies in Turner syndrome. *Hormone Research* 65 (1): 47–56.

Savitz, J., M. Solms, E. Pietersen, R. Ramesar, and P. Flor-Henry. 2004. Dissociative identity disorder associated with mania and change in handedness. *Cognitive and Behavioral Neurology* 17 (4): 233–237.

Schneider, A., and G. W. Domhoff. 2005. DreamBank. Retrieved June 15, 2010, from http://www.dreambank.net/.

Seligman, R., and L. J. Kirmayer. 2008. Dissociative experience and cultural neuroscience: Narrative, metaphor and mechanism. *Culture, Medicine and Psychiatry* 32 (1): 31–64.

Serafetinides, E.A. 1965. The EEG effects of LSD-25 in epileptic patients before and after temporal lobectomy. *Psychopharmacologia* 7 (6): 453–460.

Siddle, R., G. Haddock, N. Tarrier, and E. B. Garagher. 2002. Religious delusions in patients admitted to hospital with schizophrenia. *Social Psychiatry and Psychiatric Epidemiology* 37 (3): 130–138.

Smeets, T., M. Jelicic, and H. Merckelbach. 2006. Reduced hippocampal and amygdalar volume in dissociative identity disorder: Not such clear evidence. *American Journal of Psychiatry* 163 (9): 1643; author reply, 1643–1644.

Smith, M. 2008. Psychological correlates of mystical experience: Personality, absorption, and dissociativity. *Dissertation Abstracts International* 68 (9): 6281B. Retrieved June 15, 2010, from from Dissertations and Theses database.

Spanos, N. P., H. J. Stam, H. L. Radtke, and M. E. Nightingale. 1990. Absorption in imaginings, sex-role orientation, and the recall of dreams by males and females. *Journal of Personality Assessment* 44 (3): 277–282.

Sykes, B. 2003. *Adam's curse: A future without men.* New York: W. W. Norton.

Trimble, M., and A. Freeman. 2006. An investigation of religiosity and the Gastaut-Geschwind syndrome in patients with temporal lobe epilepsy. *Epilepsy and Behavior* 9 (3): 407–414.

Trivers, R. L. 1974. Parent-offspring conflict. *American Zoologist* 14 (1): 249–264.

Tsai, G. E., D. Condie, M.-T. Wu, and I.-W. Chang. 1999. Functional magnetic resonance imaging of personality switches in a woman with dissociative identity disorder. *Harvard Review of Psychiatry* 7:119–122.

Vaitl, D., N. Birbaumer, J. Gruzelier, G. Jamieson, B. Kotchoubey, A. Kubler, et al. 2005. Psychology of altered states of consciousness. *Psychological Bulletin* 131 (1): 98–127.

Vermetten, E., C. Schmahl, S. Linder, R. J. Loewenstein, and J. D. Bremner. 2006. Hippocampal and amygdalar volumes in dissociative identity disorder. *American Journal of Psychiatry* 163:630–636.

Walker, J. R. 1991. *Lakota belief and ritual.* Edited by R. J. DeMaille and E. A. Jahner. Lincoln: University of Nebraska Press.

Weber, P. J. 2009. Otty Sanchez, woman accused of killing newborn, ate brain: Police. July 27. Accessed June 15, 2010 from http://www.huffingtonpost.com/2009/07/27/otty-sanchez-woman-accuse_n_245627.html.

Weis, S., and M. Hausmann. 2010. Sex hormones: Modulators of interhemispheric inhibition in the human brain. *Neuroscientist* 16 (2): 132–138.

Recommended Reading

Adler, J. A. 2002. *Chinese religious traditions*. Upper Saddle River, NJ: Prentice Hall.

Aina, O. F., and O. O. Famuyiwa. 2007. *Ogun Oru*: A traditional explanation for nocturnal neuropsychiatric disturbances among the Yoruba of southwest Nigeria. *Transcultural Psychiatry* 44 (1): 44–54.

Almond, P. C. 2004. *Demonic possession and exorcism in early modern England: Contemporary texts and their cultural contexts*. Cambridge: Cambridge University Press.

Amorth, F. G. 1999. *An exorcist tells his story*. Translated by N. V. Mackenzie. San Francisco: Ignatius Press.

Baines, J., L. H. Lesko, and D. P. Silverman. 1991. *Religion in Ancient Egypt: Gods, myths, and personal practice*. Edited by B. E. Shafer. Ithaca, NY: Cornell University Press.

Berthrong, J. H., and E. N. Berthrong. 2000. *Confucianism: A short introduction*. Oxford: Oneworld Publications.

Boddy, J. 1994. Spirit possession revisited: Beyond instrumentality. *Annual Review of Anthropology* 23:407–434.

Boyce, M. 2001. *Zoroastrians: Their religious beliefs and practices*. New York: Routledge.

Buckler, F. W. 1934. Regnum et ecclesia. *Church History* 3 (1): 16–40.

Buckley, J. 1955. A note on the kingship of Christ. *Folklore* 66 (4): 410–412.

Burkert, W. 1985. *Greek religion*. Translated by J. Raffan. Cambridge: Harvard University Press.

Burkert, W. 1987. *Homo Necans: The anthropology of ancient Greek sacrificial ritual and myth*. Berkeley: University of California Press.

Carrithers, M. 1996. *Buddha: A very short introduction*. Oxford: Oxford University Press.

Castillo, R. J. 1994. Spirit possession in South Asia, dissociation or hysteria? Part I: Theoretical background. *Culture, Medicine and Psychiatry* 18:1–21.

Chajes, J. H. 2003. *Between worlds: Dybbuks, exorcists, and early modern Judaism*. Philadelphia: University of Pennsylvania Press.

Coe, M. 1999. *The Maya*. 6th ed. New York: Thames and Hudson.

Cunliffe, B., ed. 2001. *The Oxford illustrated history of prehistoric Europe*. Oxford illustrated histories. New ed. New York: Oxford University Press.

Dawson, R. 2003, trans. *The Analects*. Oxford: Oxford University Press.

De Letter, P. J. 1961. Christ the King. *The Furrow* 12 (8): 474–483.

Edson, G. 2009. *Masks and masking: Faces of tradition worldwide*. Jefferson, NC: McFarland and Co.

Egan, M. F. 1936. Christ the King. *The Irish Monthly* 64 (760): 667–672.

Falola, T., and A. Genova, eds. 2005. *Orisa: Yoruba gods and spiritual identity in Africa and the Diaspora*. Trenton, NJ: Africa World Press.

Feeley-Harnik, G. 1985. Issues in divine kingship. *Annual Review of Anthropology* 14:273–313.

Ferracuti, S., R. Sacco, and R. Lazzari. 1996. Dissociative trance disorder: Clinical and Rorschach findings in ten persons reporting demon possession and treated by exorcism. *Journal of Personality Assessment* 66 (3): 525–539.

Fiedel, S. 1992. *Prehistory of the Americas*. 2nd ed. Cambridge: Cambridge University Press.

Fingarette, H. 1972. *Confucius: The secular as sacred*. New York: Harper Torchbooks.

Foltz, R. C. 2004. *Spirituality in the land of the noble: How Iran shaped the world's religions*. Oxford: Oneworld Publications.

Foster, B. 1994. *Heart drum: Spirit possession in the Garifuna communities of Belize*. Belize: Cubola Productions.

Gahlin, L. 2002. *Egypt: Gods, myths and religion*. New York: Barnes and Noble.

Gaw, A. A., Q.-Z. Ding, R. E. Levine, and H.-F. Gaw. 1998. The clinical characteristics of possession disorder among 20 Chinese patients in the Hebei Province of China. *Psychiatric Services* 49:360–365.

Goldman, M. 2007. How to learn in an Afro-Brazilian spirit possession religion: Ontology and multiplicity in Candomblé. In *Learning religion: Anthropological approaches*, ed. D. Berliner and R. Sarró, 103–119. New York: Berghahn Books.

Goodman, F., J. H. Henney, and E. Pressel. 1974. *Trance healing and hallucination: Three field studies in religious experience*. New York: Wiley.

Guiley, R. E. 2009. *The encyclopedia of demons and demonology*. New York: Checkmark Books.

Hammond-Tooke, W. 1989. *Rituals and medicines: Indigenous healing in South Africa*. Johannesburg: A.D. Donker.

Hayden, B. 1987. Alliances and ritual ecstasy: Human responses to resource stress. *Journal for the Scientific Study of Religion* 26 (1): 81–91.

Hitchcock, J. T., and R. L. Jones, eds. 1976. *Spirit possession in the Nepal Himalayas*. Warminster: Aris and Phillips Ltd.

Hollan, D. 2000. Culture and dissociation in Toraja. *Transcultural Psychiatry* 37 (4): 545–559.

Hooke, S. H., ed. 1958. *Myth, ritual, and kingship: Essays on the theory and practice of kingship in the ancient Near East and in Israel*. Oxford: Clarendon Press.

Hopkins, T. J. 1971. *The Hindu religious tradition*. Belmont, CA: Wadsworth Publishing.

Huxley, A. 1952. *The devils of Loudun*. New York: Carroll and Graf Publishers.

Jilek-Aall, L. 1999. *Morbus Sacer* in Africa: Some religious aspects of epilepsy in traditional cultures. *Epilepsia* 40 (3): 382–386.

Kramer, F. 1993. *The red fez: Art and spirit possession in Africa*. Translated by M. Green. New York: Verso.

Lambek, M. 1981. *Human spirits: A cultural account of trance in Mayotte*. Cambridge: Cambridge University Press.

Larsen, K. 2008. *Where humans and spirits meet: The politics of rituals and identified spirits in Zanzibar*. New York: Berghahn Books.

Lewis, I. M. 2003. *Ecstatic religion: A study of shamanism and spirit possession*. New York: Routledge.

Lommel, A. 1967. *Shamanism: The beginnings of art*. New York: McGraw-Hill.

Lommel, A. 1970. *Masks: Their meaning and function.* New York: Excalibur.

Mack, J., ed. 1994. *Masks and the art of expression.* London: Harry N. Abrams.

Mageo, J. M., and A. Howard, eds. 1996. *Spirits in culture, history and mind*. London: Routledge.

Makris, G. 2000. *Changing masters: Spirit possession and identity construction among slave descendants and other subordinates in the Sudan*. Evanston, IL: Northwestern University Press.

McNamara, P. 2009. *The neuroscience of religious experience*—A response to the Ruyan-Kreitzer review. *Christian Scholar's Review,* 479–481.

Meyer, M. W., ed. 1987. *The ancient mysteries: A sourcebook: Sacred texts of the mystery religions of the ancient Mediterranean world*. San Francisco: HarperCollins.

Miller, K. 1985. *Doubles: Studies in literary history*. Oxford: Oxford University Press.

Milner, G. 1998. *The Cahokia kingdom*. Washington, DC: Smithsonian Institution Press.

Nabokov, I. 2000. *Religion against the self: An ethnography of Tamil rituals.* Oxford: Oxford University Press.

Napier, A. D. 1986. *Masks, transformation, and paradox*. Los Angeles: University of California Press.

Nevadomsky, J., and D. E. Inneh. 1983. Kinship succession rituals in Benin. 1: Becoming a crown prince. *African Arts* 17 (1): 47–54, 87.

Ng, B.-Y., and Y.-H. Chan. 2004. Psychosocial stressors that precipitate dissociative trance disorder in Singapore. *Australian and New Zealand Journal of Psychiatry* 38:426–432.

Ng, B.-Y. 2000. Phenomenology of trance states seen at a psychiatric hospital in Singapore: A cross-cultural perspective. *Transcultural Psychiatry* 37: 560–579.

Oliver, R. 2000. *The African experience*. 2nd ed. Madison: University of Wisconsin Press.

Oser, F., and H. Reich. 1990. Moral judgment, religious judgment, world view and logical thought: A review of their relationship. Part two. *British Journal of Religious Education* 12 (3): 172–181.

Owens, D'A., and B. Hayden. 1997. Prehistoric rites of passage: A comparative study of transegalitarian hunter-gatherers. *Journal of Anthropological Archaeology* 16:121–161.

Quigley, D. 2000. The killing of kings and ordinary people. *Journal of the Royal Anthropological Institute* 6 (2): 237–254.

Parsons, W. 1936. Separation of church and state. *The Irish Monthly* 64 (757): 462–466.

Pernet, N. 1992. *Rituals masks: Deceptions and revelations.* Colombia: University of South Carolina Press.

Rasmussen, S. J. 1995. *Spirit possession and personhood among the Kel Ewey Tuareg.* Cambridge: Cambridge University Press.

Rosik, C. H. 2004. Possession phenomena in North America: A case study with ethnographic, psychodynamic, religious and clinical implications. *Journal of Trauma and Dissociation* 5 (1): 49–76.

Ruskin, R. 2007. Possession. *American Journal of Psychiatry* 164 (7): 1014–1015.

Sharp, L. A. 1993. *The possessed and the dispossessed: Spirits, identity, and power in a Madagascar migrant town.* Berkeley: University of California Press.

Sharp, L. A. 1999. Exorcists, psychiatrists, and the problems of possession in northwest Madagascar. In *Across the boundaries of belief: Contemporary issues in the anthropology of religion*, ed. M. Klass and M. Weisgrau, 163–210. Boulder, CO: Westview Press.

Silverstein, T. 1939. The throne of the Emperor Henry in Dante's paradise and the mediaeval conception of Christian kingship. *Harvard Theological Review* 32 (2): 115–129.

Smith, F. M. 2006. *The self possessed: Deity and spirit possession in South Asian literature and civilization.* New York: Columbia University Press.

Somer, E., and M. Saadon. 2000. Stambali: Dissociative possession and trance in a Tunisian healing dance. *Transcultural Psychiatry* 37 (4): 580–600.

Sorensen, E. R. 2002. The temple of God, the house of the unclean spirit: Possession and exorcism in the New Testament and early Christianity. *Dissertation Abstract International* 62 (10): 3435A. UMI No. 3029539. Retrieved June 16, 2010, from Dissertations and Theses database.

Speel, C. J., II. 1963. Theological concepts of magistracy: A study of Constantinus, Henry VIII, and John F. Kennedy. *Church History* 32 (2): 130–149.

Stevens, G. B. 1890. Suggestions for the study of Paul's teaching regarding the person and work of Christ in the Epistles of the imprisonment (Colossians, Ephesians and Philippians). *The Old and New Testament Student* 11 (1): 31–33.

Todd, J., and K. Dewhurst. 1955. The double: Its psycho-pathology and psycho-physiology. *Journal of Nervous and Mental Disease* 122:47–77.

Walker, S. S. 1972. *Ceremonial spirit possession in Africa and Afro-America: Forms, meanings, and functional significance.* Leiden: Brill.

Ward, C. A., and M. H. Beaubrun. 1980. The psychodynamics of demon possession. *Journal for the Scientific Study of Religion* 19:201–207.

Watson, R. I., Jr. 1973. Investigation into deindividuation using a cross-cultural survey technique. *Journal of Personality and Social Psychology* 25 (3): 342–345.

Weiss, D. H. 1995. Architectural symbolism and the decoration of the Ste.-Chapelle. *The Art Bulletin* 77 (2): 308–320.

Winks, R. W., and S. P. Mattern-Parkes. 2004. *The ancient Mediterranean world: From the Stone Age to A.D. 600*. New York: Oxford University Press.

Wood, M. 2007. *Possession, power and the new age: Ambiguities of authority in neoliberal societies*. Hampshire: Ashgate.

Index

About the Author

PATRICK MCNAMARA, PhD, is Associate Professor of Neurology and Psychiatry at Boston University School of Medicine (BUSM) and is Director of the Evolutionary Neurobehavior Laboratory in the Department of Neurology at the BUSM and the VA New England Healthcare System. He is also Series Editor for the Praeger series Brain, Behavior, and Evolution. Upon graduating from the Behavioral Neuroscience Program at Boston University in 1991, he trained at the Aphasia Research Center at the Boston VA Medical Center in neurolinguistics and brain-cognitive correlation techniques. He then began developing an evolutionary approach to problems of brain and behavior and currently is studying the evolution of the frontal lobes, the evolution of the two mammalian sleep states (REM and NREM), and the evolution of religion in human cultures.